BUZZ
STORIES
at Thirty Thousand Feet

BY
David Price AIA & Friends

Casa Flamingo Literary Arts
NASHVILLE, TENNESSEE, USA

Published by Casa Flamingo Literary Arts, Nashville, Tennessee
www.casaflamingo.com

Paperback first printing, September 2018

ISBN: 978-0-9967504-3-1
Library of Congress Control Number: 2018952578

Cover Artwork: David A. Price
Text and Interior Design: Jennifer Wright
Copy Editor and Production Director: Tim O'Brien
Distribution: Ingram Global Publisher Service

For additional copies of "Buzz Stories at Thirty Thousand Feet" ask your local bookstore to order or purchase online at www.TheBuzzWay.com or www.amazon.com. Distributed by Ingram and available throughout the US, Canada, Australia, United Kingdom, European Union, and Russia.

———————————————

This book is dedicated to the lifelong relationship
of trust that bonded Walt & Roy Disney and
Harrison "Buzz" Price allowing contemporaries,
future generations and "Yes If" problem solvers
to find their purpose and inspiration turning
impossible dreams into realities for families,
children and people to enjoy
around the world.

———————————————

Contents

———————————————

Foreword

BY Monty Lunde, Founder of the TEA

I must admit, I was surprised when I received a call from David Price asking if I would write the forward to a book he was developing about his father, Harrison "Buzz" Price. As a further confession, though I started my career many years ago as a Disney employee and was a fellow Stanford graduate (30 years after Buzz received his MBA), I didn't even know who Buzz Price was until the mid-'90s. That said, our paths did cross and I experienced Buzz's acute cognitive abilities, mixed with a devil-may-care way of expressing himself. Sometimes intimidating, sometimes educational, always entertaining!

My story of meeting Buzz is different than most since it is not project related. It begins while I was deeply involved with the Themed Entertainment Association (TEA), a professional association representing the creators of incredible guest experiences. One of the TEA's mandates and a consistent request from the organization's members was to find a way to secure professional credits for companies and individuals who design and produce Themed Entertainment and related attractions.

Long before the inception of the TEA, companies and individuals have often been contractually precluded from advertising or promoting themselves using images or statements about projects they worked on for major entertainment companies. I'm told this began with Walt Disney's belief that all who worked on his movies and theme parks were employees of The Walt Disney Company and therefore the only name that should be associated with these projects was the company namesake, Disney. As such, the animators, concept artists, theme park creators and countless other individuals who made the Disney magic could not put their names on their designs, artwork or items the public might see. This practice was eventually adopted by other major entertainment companies and became the norm for the Themed Entertainment industry. This restriction logically carried to all outside firms and individuals (TEA members) who worked on projects for these major entertainment companies.

To help provide some public credit to the dedicated and highly talented companies and individuals designing and fabricating the world's most exceptional themed experiences, the TEA developed the

Thea Awards (named after the Greek Goddess of light and mother of the sun, moon and dawn). This awards program was envisioned to be an annual black-tie gala of a magnitude much like the Academy Awards, with equal esteem. The million-dollar question was; How do we start the event and get industry professionals to take notice and appreciate the significance of the award? This brings me to how I got to know Buzz Price.

A small committee was formed to envision what was to become the Thea Awards and establish the event as THE annual gala for the TEA. The group consisted of myself, Pat Scanlon, Barry Howard, Jeremy Railton and Bob Rogers. Though the eventual goal was to provide awards for the best attractions, themed venues, and related industry projects, a parallel goal was to create a program that (strongly) encouraged the owners and developers of major attractions to provide credit to those who worked on their projects and make those credits public in the Thea Awards program.

Since our small committee had no ability or method to receive submissions and judge them, we determined the best way to establish the validity and significance of the Thea Awards was to select an individual to receive the very first Thea Award, as a Lifetime Achievement Award. This person's reputation as a professional, leader and mentor within the industry needed to be without question. Indeed, the first Thea gala and award had to be centered on a single person who epitomized excellence and a lifetime of leadership in the industry.

I believe Pat was the first to suggest Buzz as the logical recipient of the very first Thea and proceeded to expound on Buzz's many incredible attributes and successes. Once Buzz's name was floated, all began to tell their Buzz stories and agreed he was the perfect person to establish the credibility of the Thea Awards (yes, we were planning to ride on Buzz's coattails!). At that time, I had never met or worked with Buzz and only knew of his achievements though the stories others on the committee told.

After Pat called Buzz and assured him the award was not a joke, and allayed Buzz's fears that very few would show up for the evening, a date was set for what would be a seminal event for the TEA. The 1994 Thea Awards Gala was held at the Beverly Wilshire Hotel, in Los Angeles, and attended by over 300 true admirers of Buzz Price. The evening was a parade of industry elites and personalities, all extoling Buzz's virtues and their life experiences with him. To say the evening had colorful moments would be an understatement. All were in good humor and with warm laughter and genuine love for someone who was a pioneer and influenced so many at Disney and countless other Themed Entertainment projects. I was the last on stage and as the Founder of the TEA, I presented Buzz with the Thea trophy (all 15 pounds!) recognizing Buzz's lifetime of incredible achievements. This was the very moment I first met Buzz in person!

To build the Thea committee with credible individuals, one of the stipulations (though somewhat tongue-in-cheek) was that all Lifetime Achievement recipients automatically became lifetime members of the Thea committee, thus adding gravitas and industry wisdom to the award selection committee each year. Over the last 24 years, there are only two Lifetime Achievement recipients who have actually served on the Thea committee for the remainder of their lives; Buzz Price (1994-2010) and Marty Sklar (1995-2017).

Though both had very busy lives professionally, philanthropically and personally, they committed eight weeks each year to review and help select the next group of Thea recipients, with submissions now counting over 300! Why were they so committed to a program that really didn't enhance their personal reputations? I believe it was because they understood the importance of the stories and experiences created by Themed Entertainment professionals and how vital it was to celebrate those that produced these exceptional events and attractions. They also believed in being mentors and pushing the industry forward through their influence and belief in the next generation.

What I learned about Buzz, after being with him for 14 years on the Thea committee, was that he was one of the smartest, most articulate and (at times) most irreverent people I knew in the industry. He was just as likely to say something was crap as he was to expound on the virtues of a project others overlooked. He was an intellectual, but more importantly, he was an expert at getting people to listen. Buzz had a distinctive voice and colorful rhythm to his speech that you could not ignore, or forget. He was far more than the "numbers guy" who determined the locations for Disneyland and Walt Disney World. Buzz knew his numbers as the following stories highlight, but he also had deep knowledge about what attracts and excites humans of all cultures.

In his final years, Buzz could no longer drive himself to the weekly Thea meetings so his wife, Anne, would drive him from their home in Palm Springs and patiently read a book in the BRC library while Buzz attended each four to five hour meeting. I believe Anne did this because she knew how important it was for Buzz to continue to push the industry he helped create. Even with his hearing failing, Buzz reviewed the submissions and made articulate comments, though some suspected he turned off his hearing aid when not interested in what others were droning on about.

Buzz was always committed to the success of his family, clients, friends and associates. He possessed infallible logic and was a truly unique individual, in an industry of unique individuals. After his passing in 2010, the Thea Lifetime Achievement Award was rightly renamed in Buzz's honor because he epitomized what the award stands for.

Buzz is the personification of a life well lived!

Monty Lunde
President
Technifex

Preface

I've endeavored to pull together a few stories about my late father – Harrison A. Price (1921 – 2010). He was "Buzz" Price to colleagues and friends. The recognized dean of entertainment attraction consulting. The compilation is entitled "Buzz Stories at Thirty Thousand Feet." Why the title? In part because those that worked with Buzz often met up with him at the airport before departing on a Harrison Price Company (HPC) charrette assignment. Shared airtime, travel and work left stories that linger, and it's hoped that the reader gains insight and enjoyment from the memories that are shared at high altitude and on the ground.

On one such trip Buzz penned a letter to God on a flight between Minneapolis and Los Angeles that is shared below:

Presentation to God Almighty

It is my pleasure if not my choice to be here and submit my credentials for your consideration. At the outset I would like to express my admiration for the valiant attempt you have made to provide parameters for human behavior and systems for social organization in what is no doubt one of the most complex enterprises ever undertaken by an entity.

My presentation is organized very simply around + factors and – factors inexorably accrued during my 30,000 days on earth. I will pursue a bottom line assessment which could be defined as my personal EBETKG, "evaluation before entering the Kingdom of God."

As a preface before any judgments are processed I would like to point out that some of your own precepts may be pertinent – for example, "Judge not lest you be judged." Granted that your quest is selfless, and your motives are beyond reproach, however, let me point out what you already know.

(1) Man has not picked up on some of your best guidelines, i.e., "it is nobler to give than to receive." You have failed to sell some very important and sound messages.

(2) You continue to wipe out and destroy some of our best products to the point where it is commonly said that "only the good die young."

(3) No one is minding the store regarding global resource and environmental management.

(4) You have played one ethnic off against another until almost everyone realizes that some kind of cosmic joke is at play.

(5) For millenniums and recent eons, you have underused the wisdom of women and left the fate of the world in the hands of ego-driven men.

(6) You have allowed a creeping materialism to overwhelm the simple virtues that more often prospered in earlier times.

This in not to carp but merely to point out before you assess my EBETKG that we share certain failures in behavior and performance and that your old saws about not throwing the first stone and not calling the kettle black are relevant.

So now I will file my own brief without benefit of outside counsel because I believe that style to be more to your liking and because I could not find a good lawyer here willing to take my case on contingency.

On the plus side – I always read the best funnies first – let me submit the following:

> I love my children and further their interest throughout my life.

> I adored my wife with an abiding passion and cleaved to her damn near all the time.

> I honored and love my mother and father.

> In all my working days I strove to stimulate those around me to produce and achieve to the maximum with a profound but unproved faith in the soundness of that approach.

> The medium of my message throughout my life was humor and celebration. Admittedly there are other approaches worthy of your approval, but this one was essential to me and I have suspicion that you are basically the same way and that you understand this need and have given it your OK.

> I have not gone through life unaware of the great statements of your favorite artists – your spokespersons as it were: Mozart, Beethoven, Brahms, Back, Berlioz, Schubert, Prokofiev, Stravinsky, Debussy, Faure, Verdi, and a hundred others. Your message has been heard and venerated.

Against that joyful expression of a full and happy life is the debit inventory – the list of failures – the list of indulgences, the takings, the selfishness that pervade the human system like plaque. The list is long and tough to deal with without the help of a good librarian and the Dewey Decimal System. On earth we put up a good front and we hide our failures behind a canvas. It is only up here in the moment of truth that we admit that Dorian Gray is really right out front with nothing to hide behind. Categories of failure? Courage. Purity. Bravery, Ethical Behavior, Narcissism. Shit man, you know this list better than I do.

Let us save some time and process this case through your computer. I hope I come out positive even if it is by one point in double overtime.

As a final thought, I enjoyed my time to the hilt and wish to thank you for it. If you can see fit to keep me active in an ongoing role – perhaps as a consultant on some of your many problem areas – that would be fine with me. I am good at sorting out complex problems. My rates are modest and with you I would not request any advance deposit.

With admiration and hopefulness,

Harrison Alan Price
June 21, 1988
(one week after a positive cancer biopsy)
Northwest Flight 301 Minneapolis to Los Angeles
(two sheets to the wind)

Harrison "Buzz" Price, HPC Office, Torrance, CA, '90s

"Guessing is dysfunctional, ignoring prior experience is denial. Using valid numbers to project performance is rational."
– Buzz Price

CHAPTER 1

Beyond the Numbers

BY David A. Price AIA

My father, Harrison "Buzz" Price was excellent at crunching numbers in his head. Not everyone of course can accomplish such a task, but he was a wizard at it. Great gift to have when you're in the middle of a planning session and you're putting numbers up on the white board to stimulate and help focus discussion. He could also pause and draw you into the calculus.

Dad often said, "It's all about the numbers" and his passing in 2010 certainly has not changed that perspective. For industry practitioners that worked closely with Buzz, we recall those "Buzz Moments" when WE were able to see the numbers as he saw them in real time. Those moments often occurred during an intense multi-disciplined two-day planning charrette to address preliminary economic feasibility and concept development potential for various assignments involving themed entertainment projects. Most proceedings occurred at away locations (close to the client or subject site) and flying across country or overseas was not uncommon.

Often beginning with a blank page at the start of a planning charrette, our deliberations would conclude with preliminary recommendations that addressed key market and economic parameters and an articulation of a narrative concept and program. Those experiences are filled with memories and a collective recognition that Buzz instilled in each of us the confidence that we could land the plane despite flying high with ideas and vision.

Dad is now gone, but the use of the charrette and his technique of using numbers to explain just about everything while planning for an entertainment venue are still used. They are as effective today as they were during his prime.

Buzz is also fondly remembered for having ushered in several generations of econ consultants who continue to carry the torch and mantra, "It's all about the numbers." Buzz clearly understood that, "While using valid numbers to project performance is rational," we still need to channel our utmost alchemist strengths, drawing from our talent and collective experiences and demonstrated good sense and hard work.

Buzz always said that "The key to success is the rapport and skill of the charrette team. Informed people who enjoy the process make it work." Being a part of this exclusive group who worked closely with Buzz over the years represented my post-graduate education. It's where I stepped further into the attractions world as a professional architect and strategic thinker and came to really know and appreciate my father professionally.

I count all of those I came to know during the HPC charrette era as friends, colleagues and mentors. Several have gladly shared their stories about Buzz and we have gathered them in "Buzz Stories at Thirty Thousand Feet." Each knew Buzz in their own special way.

> **Bob Rogers** worked extensively with Buzz on various attraction projects and knew him as a fellow inductee of IAAPA Hall of Fame, fellow recipient of the TEA Lifetime Achievement Award (later to be renamed after my father), and who steadfastly encouraged my father to write his book, "Walt's Revolution! By the Numbers."

> **Mike Lee**, designer, and **Pat Scanlon**, producer were frequent charrette panelists who traveled extensively with Buzz on a wide assortment of attractions-oriented assignments and who I came to know as talented collaborators and friends.

> **Jill Bensley** and **Sharon Dalrymple** were women that entered the arena of economic consulting at a time when few women did so and crafted their professional reputations beginning at ERA and later at HPC, each while working closely with Buzz. Jill would later launch her own successful economic consulting firm, JB Consulting.

> **Adam Krivatsy** first met Buzz during the early planning stages of Walt Disney World and later become a key strategic development advisor to Buzz and his clients for wide ranging destination properties in North America and Asia. Adam became my dear friend and colleague whose mentoring and encouragement brought dimension to my professional life.

> **Barry Howard**, renowned exhibition designer and planner, worked with Buzz on numerous museum related projects. What

I learned from Barry about attraction and museum planning was akin to a post-graduate crash course early in my career.

› Michael Mitchell retained Buzz to consult on the early planning for a World's Fair that did not happen (originally planned to coincide with Alaska's Statehood Anniversary). Through Buzz's recommendation to Peter Ueberroth, Michael would later join the 1984 Los Angeles Olympic Organizing Committee as Group Vice-President of Planning and Control (finance).

› Nick Winslow worked with Buzz for five decades and knew him as a relative, boss and partner, later becoming his client. I first worked with Nick during the early days of HPC on the Mount St. Helens National Park Study for the Department of Commerce & Economic Development and later on when he was at Warner Brothers on a thematic design concept for an entertainment city resort in Las Vegas, Nevada.

All have shared their personal stories. "Buzz Stories at Thirty Thousand Feet" ends with my own experience growing up with my father, later working with him as an architect and along the way forging relationships with an amazing group of colleagues, friends and mentors. I came to know my father best by working with him where the personal relationship gave way to a professional understanding and appreciation for this special man.

I also remember laughing with Dad 'til the eyes cried and the stomach ached while heading home at thirty thousand feet returning from Japan, China or Indochina. There will never be another Buzz Price, but he has left a part of himself in those who knew him and worked with him. It's where life lessons were learned – for many of us.

The Wit and Wisdom of Buzz Price

BY Bob Rogers

We had raced through the rain to the airport but missed our original flight home because a difficult charrette had gone overtime. But while re-routing our flights Buzz had sweet talked the woman behind the counter into upgrading us both into first class without an extra charge. Our plane pushed back and taxied for takeoff. Buzz ordered a double scotch on the rocks as he listened to me complaining about the last two days spent with our mutual client. Buzz and I had invented one good idea after another, only to have our client consistently select the options least likely to succeed. As our plane accelerated down the runway and began climbing, so did my venting. He listened quietly.

Now he looked at me while squinting one eye. He often did that when about to say something pithy and amazing. "You know, people pay me a lot of money to tell them what I think. For what I'm about to tell you, I should probably charge you a lot of money so that you will value it and believe it."

His drink arrived. "But I'm going to take a chance and just give it to you. Here it is: Don't fight; sell."

With that, he drained his scotch in one long draw, put his seat back and went to sleep.

Over our years working together I witnessed a lot of deep wisdom from Buzz, but none better than that. He had a way of saying what should not be said in just the right way to convince you to do what should be done.

Another example: Together we were working for a tough old self-made multi-millionaire developer on a project in Ohio – a blue collar guy who quit school after repeating the fifth grade three times and then from nothing built a $100 million dollar a year company. Our client and Buzz were both in their mid-'70s. Buzz had just delivered his opinion of the likely attendance, but the client didn't like the numbers Buzz was giving him – far lower than expected.

"Why should I believe anything you say?" said the developer.

Buzz paused, closed one eye and studied our client for a moment. Then he said, "Because I'm old and I'm gonna die soon and I don't give a shit."

The surprised client thought for a couple seconds and then said, "Well, that's a pretty damned straight answer." After that the project went forward based on Buzz's numbers.

He could be brutally honest, only caring about the right answer. One time I invited him to help us kick off a three-month project creating the conceptual design for a mystery project in Arizona. About two minutes into the first hour of the first day of a two-day kick-off meeting, the client introduced the up-to-then-secret project, revealing it would be an indoor 60-acre amusement park in Phoenix.

"Eaah. Phoenix. It's a crock of shit," said Buzz, leaping to his feet. He went to the dry erase board and in absolutely a brilliant five minutes – a true tour de force – spelled out all the numbers conclusively proving that the greater Phoenix market could never support the high construction costs and subsequent high air conditioning costs of enclosing an entire theme park, made all the worse by highly seasonal attendance patterns. "You will lose your shirt." Then he sat down. No one spoke. The stunned client silently stared at the board for about a minute, then rose to profusely thank Buzz for having saved her several hundred million dollars. As the designer suddenly out of a job I was not equally grateful at that exact moment. The project was cancelled less than 10 minutes after its start. As we packed up and left, Buzz realized I was disappointed. "Hey, you don't want to work on something doomed to fail, do you? Life's too short." And, of course he was right.

I wish I'd written down more of the great things Buzz said. But I did write down a few things, especially the ones that gave me insight into our art and craft. Here are a few of the better ones. Please pardon what may seem like a jumbled order. Each quote is meant to stand on its own, not as a cohesive whole.

> "Our objective is to elevate the soul, uplift the spirit and raise the bank balance." – Buzz Price

> "This is a great business now. Money doesn't get lost any more. First, of course, the employees are no longer ripping off their owners – at least not like they used to – and the owners are no longer ripping off the tax collector – at least not like they used to. More important, every penny is studied to death. Nothing happens by accident. Everything is analyzed. Everything is planned. Nothing gets lost."
> – Buzz Price, November 1997

"It is astonishing how often otherwise intelligent people use their economic feasibility study only to raise money, rather than to figure out how to make their project more successful." –
Buzz Price

"Most of what I do focuses on establishing the constraints...the limits and demands that the market puts on the projects. The creative guys hate this. They want to get to the fun stuff. They're like the guy that wants to start spray-painting his car before masking off all the chrome and glass. They start spraying all over the place and they just make a mess. Without constraints you just launch into an endless discussion, waste a lot of time and energy and end up with nothing. Constraints give you direction. They enable you to reach a solid conclusion." – Buzz Price

"When people come to me and say 'I have a great piece of property and I'd like to go into the entertainment business,' I regard them with great suspicion. If instead they say, 'I'd like to go into the entertainment business and I need help finding the right size and site for my idea,' I probably can help them." – Buzz Price

Convincing Clients

"The trick is gaining credibility with a client. It is one thing to be right. It's another thing to have the client believe it." – Buzz Price

"Clients come in a range of rationalities from 10 to zero." – Buzz Price

The Buzz Price 6x7 Technique: Buzz often said, "Knowing the right answer and convincing the client are two entirely different things." Buzz had many techniques for engaging clients in his process. For example, he would get the client to participate in the arithmetic of his presentations by working out his financial projections in front of them. Along the way Buzz would pretend to forget his 3rd grade multiplication tables and ask the client to help with a pocket calculator. "That would give you... huh... what's six times seven, someone?" As a result of helping with the arithmetic, the client ended up with a feeling of co-authorship in the conclusions, thus achieving buy-in.

This was all pure theater, of course. Buzz already knew the over-all bottom line findings before he began the charrette. But he pretended to discover the numbers and work it all out in front of them to achieve client buy-in. Even when it isn't mathematical, the rest of us can do the same thing in our own work by pausing or posing a question when the next answer is obvious. In a variation of this technique he would sometimes stop when obviously incomplete, and innocently ask, "Did I miss anything?" The client would remind him of the missing item. With this and many other engagement strategies he kept his clients involved, giving them that sense of co-authorship.

Research

You must have valid numbers. Buzz always challenged numbers provided by others and commissioned or personally conducted his own research to verify what was actually happening in comparable projects. On a couple of occasions, I followed him as he went out to personally examine the counting system used at the entrance to a comparable project that was generating numbers that didn't feel quite right to him. On one occasion we found a comparable attraction was counting everyone on the way in and counting them all a second time on the way out, thus doubling the reported visitor count. In addition, it was counting arriving and departing employees and service people as still more visitors!

> "Never believe the attendance numbers reported by any attraction that doesn't charge admission. Numbers that never have to be validated by bank receipts are pretty much always complete horse manure." – Buzz Price

Another time he said:

> "The US Park Service is very good at bird counts but very bad at people counts." – Buzz Price

Selling Your Ideas

"Don't fight; sell." – Buzz Price to Bob Rogers

"Arrogance sells." – Buzz Price, in September 1999, trying to explain why the Disney family continued to tolerate architect Frank Gehry despite never-ending delays and cost overruns during the construction of the Walt Disney Concert Hall project in Los Angeles. At the time, Buzz was a member of the opera house Board of Directors

"The traditional museum designers are, without exception, an architecturally dominated yawn." – Buzz Price

Buzz Price on the Subject of Charrettes

Buzz often did his work in front of his client, inviting his client to collaborate, He called these two-day marathons charrettes.

Here's how Buzz explained what he did in his part of our charrettes:

"The Feasibility Advisor [that's Buzz], usually together with the client, will look at the range of projects and their different penetration rates and decide where the new project would fit in to this list. How does the visitor experience of the proposed new project compare with the 'comparable' visitor experiences offered by the attractions on this list? Better than this one, not as good as that one, etc. A rational client will not say, 'We are going to beat the highest and best comparable project in the world.' They should instead be guided toward the middle of the healthy group. In a recent example regarding a space-related attraction, the National Air and Space Museum was a gravity-defying phenomenon, so it was thrown out. One might also disregard the several that were at the bottom of the range at 1 to 3% market penetration. I call those 'Candidates for Bankruptcy.' If the healthy middle group ranged from 6 to 11%, then a rational guess for the proposed new project might be about 8 or 9% market penetration, provided the proposed guest experience of the new project is comparable to those in that range of market penetration." – Buzz Price

Know the purpose. "If we understand what the client is trying to do with the charrette, we know what to do, how to staff it, what to deliver, how to time it and how to price it." – Buzz Price

Start at the end: "The secret is to create the meeting agenda with the report table of contents in mind. Then, during the meeting, you need to keep them on track, so you come home with the stuff you need in order to write the report. I used to tell my guys at ERA, 'Before you do any work on this job, write me the introduction and the table of contents of your final report.' That becomes your guide through the process. You can change it as you go, but you have to begin with the end in mind." – Buzz Price

"When we succeed, we shape up the vision of the project in a way that reduces risk and improves the odds of success for the project." – Buzz Price

"We blend economic order with conceptual wisdom." – Buzz Price

"The less experienced the client, the more they need a charrette. The more experienced the client, the more likely they are to insist on a charrette."– Buzz Price

"Larger charrette budgets, like larger charrettes, tend to be less effective. Lean and mean tends to be most effective." – Buzz Price

"Speed can increase quality. Work fast." – Buzz Price

"Don't go over budget – yours or your client's." – Buzz Price

Evaluating a Charrette

Was the charrette successful? Here is Buzz Price's three-way test:

1. Did the client like it?
   A. The process?
   B. The result?
   C. Did we get paid?
2. Did it come in on budget?
3. Did we consider the result to be of good quality and responsible to the task?

Of these, number one is most important, especially the part about getting paid.

Story

"We have a product that is very important to society – manufactured fun for the masses. What is increasingly missing are relevance and intelligence." – Buzz Price, November 1997

It isn't all about market sizes and comparables.

"The creative concept expands or contracts the achievable." – Buzz Price

"The audience is fickle. They expect and demand a quality product and quality service. Short change the story, the investment or the operation and the audience goes elsewhere." – Buzz Price

Buzz liked doing charrettes with BRC because we would be all in the same room, BRC inventing the creative concept simultaneously with Buzz identifying and shaping the economic opportunity. He felt that if the numbers and the creative evolved together, influencing each other along the way, they produced a more successful product.

"Sometimes when you go only by the numbers, the project is impossible. When you inject the art, it becomes possible."
– Buzz Price

About story in general:

"High tech without soft touch is like sex with a robot." – Buzz Price, November 1997

"Today we are engaged in a contest between the hard edge and the soft edge. For those pursuing the hard edge it is a short step back to the parks with gum on the walk ways, trash, vandalism and young people out of control." – Buzz Price, November 1997

Attraction Operation

"The big operators must deal in big markets, so they have to ignore half the country." – Buzz Price

"Operating budgets for the subject attraction are drawn from industry experience, but also incorporate judgments and assumptions as to the requirements of the proposed operation; fine-tuning will be needed once the attraction's precise content and staffing needs have been determined. These budgets should therefore be viewed as planning objectives geared to achieving financial self-sufficiency on a commercial, for-profit basis."
– Buzz Price

"A mediocre facility with a great operation will always beat a high-tech facility with a mediocre operation." – Buzz Price

Buzz Price and I were once working on a visitor center for NASA's Jet Propulsion Laboratory, which is owned and operated by CalTech, some of the brainiest guys on the planet. These guys could create a space ship to safely land a robot on Mars or Pluto but as a part of their visitor center they wanted nothing to do with running a restaurant. Not even a muffin cart. The prospect absolutely terrified them. I guess it pays to know your core competencies and stick to them.

Buzz increased ours. Through his half-century career and through his continuing legacy of the universally-used metrics he invented and taught, he increased the core competency of our entire industry for generations to come.

Master of Numbers and Life

BY Michael Lee

The Game Was On!

It would usually begin with a phone call and his gravelly voice. "Mike, this is Buzz. What are you doing the second Tuesday of next month?" Of course, I would clear my calendar for him. "We've got an assignment in Malmo, Sweden." (Or some other faraway place) "Can I write you in? Great! See you there (click)." Short and to the point. No "how are you?" or "what's going on?"

There was never a formal contract, never a dispute; the check was always on time. It was always just pure professionalism from this genius of a man. I would fly off into the night to meet Buzz and the others he had chosen to play a serious and fun game he called the charrette. We never knew what adventure awaited us, or in what way we would be able to solve the problems presented by his clients.

All I knew was, this man was the best there had ever been! The master of numbers! I put complete faith in him and he put complete faith in us. He would build a case for success with numbers and do so with the ease of an artist painting a beautiful landscape. He knew that if he built an economic prediction properly (which I've since come to know as the box, you know, the one you must think outside of), he could trust that his numbers would then guide us to fill the box with ideas, concepts, possible guest experiences and other interesting stuff. If that stuff didn't fit into the box, the box might be modified to accommodate an idea if it had legs. The numbers informed the ideas, the ideas informed the numbers. They must work hand-in-hand! Back and forth we would go, eventually hammering out something extra-ordinary.

What was extraordinary was his juggling of difficult, complex questions, and answering them with a theatrical clarity unlike anyone else I have ever known. Like his mentor, Walt Disney, Buzz was one of a kind.

As we were concluding and looking forward to the next assignment, he would sometimes privately say thanks but tell me, "You're my secret weapon," probably to build my fledgling self-confidence...and it did! I thought he probably said that to each one who was lucky enough to call Buzz their mentor. Some things are better than money!

The Case of the Recalcitrant Billionaire

Most of the time we could solve the problems to the satisfaction of the client, except on one occasion. Buzz had been asked by Sheldon Adelson to advise him about his Las Vegas property, the Sands Hotel and Casino, which had become a sad and worn-out place. But Adelson just could not see it. We had wrestled with the problems over several days, and eventually recommended Adelson demolish the Sands and build a new themed resort in its place. The more reasons we presented, the more agitated and recalcitrant Adelson became. We listened while Buzz determinedly went head to head with one of the richest men in the world. Adelson kept trying to drive Buzz into a corner with his "Why, why, why?"

Eventually, after two days of heated debate, Buzz did something that I've only seen him do once. As Adelson asked again, "Why?" Buzz responded, "Because that's what Walter Elias Disney would have done!" Adelson was stopped dead in his tracks. He was red in the face and fuming. There was no come-back. He knew Buzz had thrown the knock-out punch. The only thing Adelson could do, he did. "You're fired!" he said. We left Las Vegas deflated, but feeling we had done the right thing. Buzz always advocated doing what was right for the success of the project, regardless of the consequence to contract or reputation. Months passed as we heard stories of some six or so other consultants having the same humiliating experience, and being likewise fired. All had recommended tearing down the Sands. All had been fired, except the very last one.

Today you might note the Venetian, one of the most successful hotel resorts in Las Vegas, stands where the Sands once was. Buzz had been right all along. Although Buzz never got the credit, he did get the satisfaction of seeing the Venetian's success before his passing. Some things are better than winning the argument.

Driving in the Night

Upon Buzz's passing, David Price recounted with a peaceful sadness, the hours before and after. He told me it had been unlike anything he had experienced before – serene, nearly magical. It made me recall a wonderful experience with David's father, my mentor, Buzz. He and I were driving to an engagement late in the night. As sometimes happens at that time, when sleep would be best, the conversation drifted to what things are important in life – the things that matter most. Buzz lovingly told me about his sweetheart Anne and recounted the days when they were young and fell in love. He told me about his love for each of his children, and how each of them had made him proud. His voice broke as he talked about his first son who had died as a little one and how he still missed him after all these years.

I knew then, this man who was known for his success in business, his acumen with numbers, rubbing shoulders with the world's elite, was also a man of faith, a devoted husband, father and grandfather. Buzz mastered what many seek in life, the joy of loving and of being loved. I count my experiences with him as some of my most cherished. Some things can be cherished forever.

Thank you Buzz!

CHAPTER 4

Life Lessons

BY Patrick Scanlon

Some of my greatest personal and professional experiences involve participating in Buzz Price charrettes. For me, Buzz's charrettes were fun and exciting and, at the same time, draining and filled with anxiety. The promise to the client was that Buzz and his team would evaluate and assess the possibilities and potentials of a client's dream to develop a project, usually a public destination of some kind (theme park, visitor center, museum, aquarium, resort, etc.,) and then provide the client with answers, analysis and recommendations in just two days. These recommendations would include a concept description, market assessment, attendance estimates, project sizing/programing, preliminary development costs and a preliminary investment viability pro forma.

The main difference in a Buzz Price charrette, as opposed to an architect's design charrette, is that Buzz dealt with a much broader pallet of development and viability issues. And, with Buzz, we always delivered answers and recommendations. We never gave ourselves the out of not providing those deliverables.

Buzz Price Charrettes

It would go something like this:

Buzz would call and say, "Are you available for a charrette on _____, in _____." Answer, "For you, Buzz? You bet. Response, "Okay, I'll send you a deposit check, and you'll get a briefing book a couple days before you leave. See you in _____." Click.

Next thing you knew, Buzz and his team were meeting at the destination airport, with each team member having read through the briefing book on the plane ride. We'd have dinner that night, have some wine, talk and laugh a bit and the next day the charrette would begin.

Buzz had a way about him in leading his charrettes. He was engaging, informed and entertaining. He always took the lead and looked to his assembled team to coalesce and contribute. Buzz was like a trapeze performer flying without a net. He placed faith and trust in his team members to make him look good. Always, we would give the client our very best effort. Together we tackled issues, reasoned solutions, complemented one another and openly disagreed at times as we explored the possibilities, obstacles and unknowns. Paramount in our group dynamic was that we never wanted to let Buzz down. We loved the man and so admired his accomplishments.

Day One

Buzz would get things started by overviewing the client's dream and then outline the agenda of how we were going to proceed. He typically did this by inserting stories of his experiences with Walt Disney or others who also had dreams. As he got things underway, there would be smiles and laughs along the way. This would get us and the client off to a good beginning. Then Buzz would talk about the market, competitive project analogs and the strengths and weaknesses of the proposed project site. After that, we'd start exploring creative concepts, often getting deep into the weeds as we'd push boundaries.

At the end of day one, it was normal for us to be in the dark as to how we could bring things together into an intelligent, cohesive result the next day. Buzz would advise the client at the beginning of the charrette that he/she/they would likely be frustrated, impatient and annoyed with us by the end of the first day, but that he hoped they would keep the faith and stick with us and show-up the next morning.

Day Two

Day two was "magic day." Buzz would start by giving a written review of the previous day's wanderings, and that review always made everyone feel much better about all that had been accomplished. That review, along with the team dinner and team meeting/work session we'd had the previous night, is what kicked off our pursuit of answers. Our charrette tradition was that the scrap of day one was the seed from which our ideas and recommendations would flower on day two. Often, we didn't have our ideas fully formed until we started day two. A spark could come from anyone. That right spark might not come right away, but we'd push until one of those sparks lit the fire that would take us home. And, amid the chaos of all the writings and numbers and drawings on the walls would come discipline, focus and inspiration. We always forced ourselves to get to the promised answers and deliverables.

That determination and tradition is what helped us to get out of our way and let the answers come.

Finally, four to six weeks after the charrette, Buzz would submit the final charrette report to the client. All of us would send Buzz our notes, drawings and writings and he'd synthesize them, along with his perspectives and numbers, into the final result.

Charrette Lessons

Participating in Buzz Price charrettes taught me many important lessons:

1. I learned to have faith and confidence in myself, that I could go into the dark unknown and find the answers I needed, one way or another, to find the light and make it bright.

2. I learned that surrounding myself with talented, capable, good people is the key to effective, creative problem solving.

3. I learned about the power of the "team," and the ability of collective team (properly selected for the task at hand with members having positive personal interaction qualities) to focus effectively and efficiently on a common purpose to create and problem solve.

4. I learned leadership skills, observing Buzz, in how to interact with a client and how to steward and energize a team to deliver for that client.

5. Most profoundly, I learned that the tradition of vaudeville is alive and well. During a charrette, Buzz would call out one of us to "take it," or he may need a break, and one of his team would stand up, go to the front and take the lead. This was done in the moment, ready or not. We did it without hesitation because all of us never wanted to let Buzz down. And, that tradition of stepping-up made each of us stronger and more capable people.

6. Finally, participating in Buzz charrettes gave me insights into myself and my inner strengths that assist me today in tackling life. I maintain a positive outlook, while in the dark in difficult situations, having faith that if I keep pressing forward I will find a solution or a solution will find me.

Thank you, Buzz. I love you dearly!

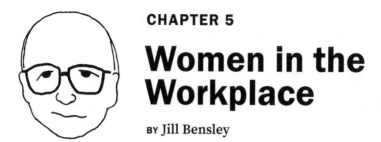

CHAPTER 5

Women in the Workplace

BY Jill Bensley

Lucky to Have Buzz at the Helm

We are at a critical moment in history right now, where men and women who have abused their power for decades are being held accountable for their overtly disgusting deeds. I grew up in a culture where women "need not apply" as consultants in the entertainment and attraction industries. And for the few of us who pushed ahead anyway, we were lucky to have Buzz at the helm.

I was a 5'6" 118 pounds, 24-year-old, freshly graduating from Berkeley in Economics, the only girl in my class. Why is this important? Because about 99.9% of my co-workers, clients and bosses were big men, mostly older than I, with an abundance of arrogance and ignorance regarding women in the workplace. Most had never met an equal with a vagina.

I had been working at Chouinard Art School, which was going through the transition to CalArts in Valencia. I got hired as assistant to the two deans of the Design School. It was great experience and I met some fascinating professionals, most of whom eventually got fired as Chouinard, a very liberal arts school, became a conservative Disney funded school. But that's a story for another time. This job of mine did not require much of a business or econ education. I got bored and started looking for a new job. And up came an ad to be a business consultant at ERA, where I knew I could use my education. After all, it was Economics Research Associates!

The Interview

My interview with Buzz began by chatting about the Chouinard/CalArts (California Institute of Arts) connection and how I got the job, what I did, did I like it, why did I leave. Buzz was on the Board of Chouinard/CalArts, and that was my in. I don't think I would have ever gotten hired otherwise. After all, I looked like his daughter and that wasn't a professional designation.

The most significant chunk of the interview went as follows (at least the parts I can remember):

"We need someone to help out our VP's, to do research, write reports and travel with them. You'll be hired as an associate."

What that was, I had no idea. But I didn't want that job. I had just gotten married and I wanted to try my hand at being a wife, being home a bit, not traveling all the time. So I said: "Don't you have any positions as assistants?" This, I thought would keep me grounded in Los Angeles. So much for "leaning in."

Buzz responded, "Why don't you want to be an associate?" Good question, why indeed!

I responded, "I just got married and I'd like to be at home a bit."

To which he said, "Well, I guess that's healthy."

How I regretted turning down the job as an associate! It would take me years to climb back up from being hired as a research assistant instead of an associate.

And so began my professional life with Buzz. We traveled the cycle of life's major events: Births, deaths, marriage, divorce, heart attacks, and broken bones. Those decades with Buzz cemented him as my mentor, a man who would yell at me, compliment me, worry about me, and brag about me. He was definitely my "work daddy" but he was also someone who profoundly understood me and could make me laugh until my cheeks were wet with tears.

Many of the stories I would like to tell you, I cannot. Those who knew Buzz understand why. He was the most inappropriate and irreverent man I knew! So, I'll clean it up and give you some one-or two-liners.

I once overheard him tell someone when describing me, "She's as good as any guy I know." Incidentally, this was the best compliment I ever received!

One bit of wisdom came from Annie, the day after I had a miscarriage and was working from home. She called me and said, "You shouldn't be working, you should take care of yourself." Coming from a family where I had neither guidance nor oversight, I appreciated her caring and wisdom.

I eventually became his trusted research person. I would do anything for him, research-wise. I often worked for him for nothing, just to get it perfect. I knew he did the same for his clients.

I worked for him on and off for 30 years. We would often fight about analytics, recommendations, writing. He made me cry a time or two

with his brutally honest assessment of my work: "This sentence is an abomination!" he opined. I learned that there is no crying in consulting!

I grew up to be a very successful economic consultant.

What I Learned from Buzz

I learned to "handle clients" or fire them when I knew they would never listen.

I learned how to write a concise and direct report, not-with-standing the copious amount of research that was presented. Regarding a briefing book I had prepared, he once said "mine is bigger than yours."

I learned to work hard, and never give up, especially when there was a result to be had.

I learned to handle a client, and to tell them what they can do, never what they can't.

I learned that laughter can be a reward in itself. Buzz would sometimes start a charrette by dunking his tie in his coffee, just to establish rapport with the client. It usually worked because it made him more approachable.

I learned to never back down but to work cooperatively

I learned to listen.

I learned THE NUMBERS. I came out of school without a hint of how to do a market/financial feasibility report. He often said, "We are numbers people." I always keep that in mind on any job, large or small.

I learned how to not take anything too seriously. He was a contrast in purpose: deadly serious and hysterically funny.

I learned how to keep a marriage fresh after 30 or 40 years, by watching him and Annie.

I learned to stand at the helm of a charrette, to run it, to keep people in line without insulting them. I was the head of my Entertainment Development Council at a prestigious industry nonprofit and ran my meetings the way I learned from watching Buzz.

I learned to get the best advice from the best, most creative and multi-disciplined experts.

I learned what's important in life, even though at times he was 100% work, no play.

As he rolled into the last decade of his life, he told me over and over that he had to go before Annie. I was there a day or two before he died. I came to say goodbye to him in the hospital. He wasn't really alert, but I sat with Annie as he said things from their past, reliving memories from when they had been a young couple.

I said goodbye and thank you. I hope he heard me.

CHAPTER 6

Gold Standard Mentor

BY Sharon Dalrymple

I met Buzz Price in 1967 when he headed Economics Research Associates (ERA), then housed in the old blue Tishman building on South Flower Street in downtown Los Angeles. I had just resigned from my first job out of college as public relations assistant to the marketing director of a major local bank. This job involved a number of writing duties, such as press releases, a gossipy employee newsletter, a quarterly puff piece for the bank's customers, and helping my boss with the annual report. All were mundane tasks that had to be completed within a rigid set of editorial guidelines laid down by an anal-retentive management committee. It took about 18 months before I reached the conclusion that the stifling culture of the banking world was not my cup of tea.

First Time Buzz Hired Me

An employment agency sent me to ERA to apply for a job as an administrative assistant, an updated term for what used to be called a Girl Friday, kind of a secretarial Jill-of-all-trades. I didn't have any experience pertinent to the field of research and consulting and had low expectations of landing the job. Much to my surprise, when I interviewed with Buzz, he hired me on the spot.

He later told me he was swayed by two factors. First, he learned that I had majored in music at UCLA and, while a student, worked as an orchestral score transcriber and gofer for distinguished American composer Roy Harris, then on the faculty. This got his attention because Buzz and his wife Anne, a former opera singer, were devoted music lovers. Secondly, he thought my background in writing on financial topics at the bank would be useful to him. He gave a lot of speeches and wanted help with those, and most proposals for consulting jobs required a qualifications package that described the firm's experience and abilities in suitably glowing prose.

In addition to aiding Buzz with writing this and that, I would work primarily as assistant to one of ERA's vice presidents. This VP was in charge of a long-term consulting program for the Kentucky State Department of Commerce that sought to recruit new industry for economically depressed counties in the state. In this capacity, I would have a chance to get my feet wet in research by putting together data of interest to companies that might want to consider Kentucky for a manufacturing plant. If I did well and liked the work, Buzz told me I could segue into a promotion to the research staff within a reasonable period. When the Kentucky contract ran out a little shy of two years later, I graduated to full-blown research assistant and began my journey up through the hierarchy of the professional staff. At about this same time, ERA relocated its offices to suburban Westwood, just down the hill from my old stomping grounds at UCLA.

Second Time Buzz Hired Me

The second time Buzz hired me came about 10 years later. In 1969, Buzz sold ERA to Planning Research Corporation (PRC), became an executive with the new parent company and, after a while, moved to corporate headquarters in Washington, DC. To make a long story short, Buzz came to regret that decision and, although he hung in there for almost a decade, ultimately severed ties with PRC. By the start of 1978, he was back in LA and on his own again.

I was quietly working at my desk one afternoon in the spring of that year when someone slipped furtively into my office and quickly closed the door. Startled, I looked up to see none other than Harrison Price. I heard he had returned to LA but hadn't seen or spoken to him since he went to Washington. He took a seat in the chair opposite my desk and leaned forward. Never one to waste time on pleasantries, he came right to the point. "I have a proposition for you." I was in a state of shock at his sudden materialization out of nowhere and found myself tongue-tied. I think I blushed and weakly stammered out, "What kind of proposition?" He chuckled and told me he had just started up a new consulting company bearing his name, working out of his home for the time being. "I booked a job where I need some research support," he said, "Maybe a week's worth of time. You'd be perfect for it. Will you moonlight it for me?"

I was flattered that he asked for my help and simultaneously a little nervous about the ethics of his request. Buzz was now a competitor of ERA, which would make me some kind of double agent if I said yes. But I did say yes and rationalized it by convincing myself I was just doing a one-time favor for the guy who gave me my start in the consulting business. I owed him. When our short meeting was over, Buzz cracked open my office door, peered cautiously into the hallway and, finding the way clear of familiar faces, made a beeline for the exit. How he managed to sneak in and out of there without being spotted by someone who knew who he was remains a mystery.

By working after office hours for several nights and coming in on a couple of Saturdays, I did the research he needed (mainly a plunder of the ERA library) and prepared some spreadsheets. He gave me a check and that was the end of it until the fall of that year. I had been growing increasingly dissatisfied with the progress of my career at ERA, too much grunt work I could do in my sleep and fewer plum assignments than were rightfully my due. When I pleaded for a change, I got a condescending pat on the head, figuratively speaking, along with what I knew was an empty promise that things would get better. I resentfully threw in the towel. This was admittedly rash given not much between me and the wolf at the door and no certainty of finding another position soon.

Naturally, Buzz was the first person I called. I told him I had left ERA and why. "Let's talk," he said, and invited me to lunch a few days hence. Buzz could charm the spots off a leopard when he wanted to, and he easily sold me on the future of my dreams at the nascent Harrison Price Company (HPC). What followed were nearly 30 years of a rewarding professional association with HPC and an enduring friendship with the dean of entertainment attraction consulting, not to mention gold-standard mentor.

HPC Charrette

It was at HPC that I was introduced to the charrette, the economic planning version of the "story board" conference originated by Walt Disney to springboard an attraction. The Disney model was strictly in-house, whereas the repurposed variety blended a team of outside experts together with a client group for a meeting of the minds. For a couple dozens of these sessions, Buzz assigned me to put together the briefing book and act as "scribe," a fancy word for note-taker and eventual author of the end-product report.

The procedure rarely varied – the format was basically a template that would be followed again and again for a diverse range of projects in manifold locations. It started with the briefing book distributed to all charrette participants, containing background site and market data that helped set the stage for the discussions, together with a charrette agenda. Then we'd all gather at the appointed conference venue for a one or (more often) two-day think session. The ultimate result was a summary report setting forth a preliminary development program and financial pro forma that enabled a go/no-go decision and jump-started subsequent formal feasibility analysis.

Buzz cherry-picked the charrette team, with the goal of getting a range of expertise and knowledge that would cross-pollinate. Depending on the project, that might mean attraction designers, real estate developers, attraction managers, land planners, and curators and other specialists in addition to economists like himself. Buzz tried to keep the size of the panels as small as possible, generally a maximum of a dozen people and a target size of seven or eight, including both the consulting team and the client representatives. Some clients wanted to include a small army of in-house staff. Buzz always reminded them of the old axiom that the amount of real business accomplished at a meeting is inversely proportional to the number of people attending. When clients balked at his limitation on size, he compromised by telling them to pick up to four key players for the panel and have the extras attend as spectators.

Not just anyone can lead a successful charrette. It takes someone who is part P.T. Barnum (showman), part General George Patton (commander), part Sigmund Freud (brain-prober), and part Mahatma Gandhi (pacifier). Buzz skillfully alternated between these personas as the situation demanded. He never let any single person, on the client side or the consultant side, dominate. As you can imagine, there were some big egos in the panel mix. This sometimes led to heated exchanges. Buzz believed that contention between participants could be effective in getting the intellectual juices flowing but was careful never to let flaring tempers get out of hand.

Buzz was a man of enormous energy and hated to interrupt the dialogue once it got rolling. Agendas always had a slot for lunch, but also included brief morning and afternoon breaks to give people a chance to stretch their legs, answer the call of nature, or phone the office, which Buzz tended to blitz right through. When I noticed group members beginning to fidget, I'd slip him a message that said, "It's pee time," and he'd reluctantly call a recess. And it was almost always a working lunch. Buzz couldn't tolerate down-time given the charrette's short duration and a bunch of expensive consultants on the clock.

The discussions were typically free-wheeling and far-ranging, especially on the first day when the group began pitching suggestions on things like theme, scale of development, means of overcoming site constraints, and other issues. With so many ideas flying, these initial sessions might have been chaotic had it not been for Buzz's talent for herding cats. He kept everyone more or less on track. The process settled down quite a lot on the second day. Once the panel had a little time to digest the first day's discussions, a relaxing dinner, and a good night's sleep, things noticeably began to gel, leading to a consensus, or occasionally, a couple of alternative development programs deemed equally viable.

With a general agreement on concept and scale, it was then Buzz's turn at bat. He ran the numbers on potential attendance, optimum project sizing, and financial performance with his customary aplomb. He was a madman with a marker pen (he especially liked the purple one), attacking the whiteboard or easel pad with gusto.

Back in the home office after the conference, I set about distilling my notes along with other notes, sketches, or diagrams contributed by other team members to create the charrette summary report. This was not a verbatim transcript of the proceedings. It was instead a summary of key findings and conclusions, backed up with some of the underpinning material contained in the briefing book and fleshed out with concept illustrations and other visuals. In the early charrettes that Buzz chaired, he tape-recorded the meeting and afterward had his secretary type it all out word for word. When he saw how much chaff obscured the wheat, he wisely abandoned this practice.

My years of working with Buzz were often joyful, occasionally nerve-wracking, and always challenging. We had our ups and downs, fortunately many more of the former than the latter. Assignments took us to places near and far, where we had both great successes as well as a few hellish misadventures I'm still trying to blot from memory. But I wouldn't trade the experience for a king's fortune. Well, maybe. If the numbers look good enough, as Buzz would say.

Special Qualities Not Often Found

BY Adam Krivatsy

Buzz had qualities you don't often find in one person – warm-hearted, smart, intelligent and creative-minded all combined with strong determination, guts and character.

My Lucky Star

Who knows how my life would have evolved if Buzz and I had not met at Kaanapali? We were introduced through a consulting agreement that ERA (Buzz' firm) had with our client Henry Walker, President of Amfac. Inc., a major property owner on the island of Maui.

My job was to coordinate the professional team responsible for convincing Maui County's elected officials and the sugar cane workers' union that the introduction of tourism would not be detrimental to the island's economy and that water requirements for irrigating sugar cane and operating a golf resort could both be satisfied.

ERA addressed the financial and fiscal implications of creating and operating the first neighbor-island vacation resort community in the State of Hawaii. Buzz saw the groundbreaking project within a broader international context – the entire South Pacific. His numbers proved that tourism would not have a detrimental effect on Maui's economy and that in the long run it would be in Maui's best interest to diversify its agricultural economy. It took another two years to secure the needed county approvals for our plans.

By 1967, we had completed our initial assignment for Amfac, Inc. That same summer, I received a call from Buzz telling me that the Disney organization was making plans for Walt Disney World in Central Florida and they needed me. Buzz was on the Disney Board. I was interested.

In short, Buzz's trust in me and my working relationship with Bob Hart led to the next chapter of my professional life – a successful consulting practice of nation-wide and international scope.

Thank you Buzz!

Back from Washington, D.C. and at the helm of his newly formed company HPC, Buzz had initiated a flourishing practice conducting planning charrettes that addressed econ feasibility and concept development potentials. His clients benefited from Buzz's in-depth understanding of the themed attraction industry, his working relationship with leading professionals and the respect and admiration he generated through collaborative team efforts. I was invited to serve as the planning and design arm of some of those charrettes in Japan, the United States and Panama.

Oita Hot Springs Retirement Community

This assignment brought us to the Oita Prefecture of Japan's Kyushu region. Our clients intended to create a golf resort community to serve big city executives and their families.

Located on a peninsula, the area was blessed with ample hot springs, was near a picturesque old fishing harbor. The hills promised potential for residential development with views to the ocean. After we had visited the site and Buzz had evaluated Oita's market potential, we were prepared to recommend development of a visitor destination centered on the hot springs, coupled with a high-end retirement community.

Buzz' proposed concept involved less financial risk, did more to appreciate our clients land values and offered a major benefit by "putting Oita on Japan's map" as a unique vacation destination. Golf could be developed on a nearby site but was not essential to the success of our clients' project.

Oita proved the success of Buzz' axiom: Keep it simple and keep financial risks to the minimum.

Kishiwada Waterfront

Established in the14th Century, Kishiwada is a medium sized (pop. <20,000) waterfront community on Osaka Bay, just a short train ride from downtown Osaka. HPC was retained to explore the commercial and recreational potential of the city's historic waterfront.

In our site visit we focused on two parallel ideas: 1) Adapting existing piers and other shoreline improvements to commercial fishing excursions and; 2) Creating a welcoming harbor for a high-end yacht club for Osaka's boating enthusiasts.

Both uses appeared promising for the drab, industrial waterfront's future use, however they were to serve mainly Osaka's seasonal markets and did little for a year-round, 24/7 use of Kishiwada's waterfront. Buzz recommended permanent waterfront housing for local residents and second home owners. The concept promised new life and added value to Kishiwada's underutilized waterfront. Today the new residential neighborhood is served by a junior high school, a beach park and an improved riverfront park connecting the waterfront to the historic downtown. A good example of Buzz' creative thinking out of the box.

Sonia Hills Wellness Resort

Another assignment took the HPC charrette team to a beautiful, mature cedar orchard planted for commercial purposes in the hills south of Kyoto. Dubbed Sonia Hills, the high altitude, sloping terrain inspired our client to consider development of a mountain resort of Bavarian architectural theme.

Walking around on the beautiful property Buzz wryly remarked, "Only a fool would cut ski runs into this unique cedar grove surrounded by miles and miles of terraced rice paddies."

So, we conceptualized a Bavarian themed resort centered on a wellness theme to be supported by an elaborate, superbly staffed spa.

Buzz was right! Snow sports are seasonal, and the site did not offer high quality runs. We planned a network of beautiful walks in the woods for year-round occupants of the resort at a time when walking trails represented the most rewarding visitor attraction. The nearly 23 million Kansai Region fueled by the urban population of Kyoto, Kobe and Nagoya could support a wellness-themed vacation destination. Thank you Buzz for saving the trees for a wellness resort!

Ginoza Beach "Resort"

This time Sumitomo Corporation sought HPC's advice in Okinawa. The site in question was a beachfront property that formerly served the US military; it was to be developed into a golf-oriented resort.

The narrow, elongated site was on the lee side of the island. Any boating access was to be created and maintained through dredging in the shallow coastal waters. The beach was beautiful, however very narrow. We noted that the north shore beaches across the island, less than four miles away were much wider, faced navigable water and spectacular surf. We also learned that on the north shore the spacious Okinawa Spa Golf Resort represented potential competition (or a potential resource?) and plans for building the equally roomy Atta Terrace Golf Resort were underway. The two nearby hotels were built on the breezy north shore of the island.

Before we were through with our site visit, Buzz remarked, "This site sucks!" Over dinner, we started speculating about how we might redeem the project. Our two-day charrette produced two alternatives: 1) Waterfront vacation housing centered on a beach club with ready access to the beach and 2) A combination of beach-oriented vacation housing and an executive golf course enhanced with many waterfront tees and holes. The numbers worked out for both alternatives, with more promise for the housing scheme.

Buzz saved the day by explaining to our clients that we only recommend projects that promise success. Location, configuration and attributes of the given site were not suitable for developing a successful golf-oriented beach resort. "There is still too much undeveloped land on the north shore of Okinawa!" Thank you Buzz for saving our team's reputation – and our clients' ass!

La Playita

In 1993 the Panama's Tourist Bureau (IPAT) retained HPC's services to conceptualize a visitor destination on Colon's historic La Playita waterfront. Although run-down due to the lack of re-investment after the departure of American troops from the Panama Canal, the site appeared to have great potential for revitalization through the Caribbean passenger cruise industry.

The place and its historic buildings along Avenida Del Frente had great potential: they faced Bahia de Limon, the protected entry to the Panama Canal and the piers were designed to accommodate ocean-going vessels. The site included the northern end station of the Panama Canal Railroad. While the historic waterfront was occupied by squatters, relocating them appeared to be only a question of some government funds. The market was there: the Caribbean Cruise industry was growing and was actively looked for new cruise destinations.

IPAT and the Caribbean Cruise Association supplied reliable numbers regarding visitor potential and visitor expenditures. Buzz's numbers looked promising, assuming that the president's office would support its Tourist Office by clearing the site of squatters.

However, government action did not materialize and the inspiring project that could have revitalized Colon's historic waterfront never happened. I was very disappointed and made many trips to work with local businessmen to resurrect our project. Buzz knew better; he reminded me that we did our best, now it is Panama's turn to run with the ball!

Twenty-five years later, La Playita is still a blemish on Panama's face. Buzz was right, "When we have done our share, it's our client's job to run with the ball."

Thank you Buzz!

CHAPTER 8

We Didn't Get the Job

BY Barry Howard

I first came to know Buzz during the 1974 Spokane World's Fair. I'm not sure how that came about, but I think it was through Petr Spurney, general manager of the expo. I'm not sure if Buzz had any significant role in the economic planning for that event, but when he saw our treatment of the science section of the US Pavilion, he immediately understood and appreciated my focus on scholarship-driven interpretive design. With his Disney history, he of course was firmly entrenched in entertainment design and themed attractions, but he quickly saw the potential for applying his economic principles to large informational exhibits and museums.

I on the other hand had no connection at all with theme parks, Disney or Universal Studios, but had begun to consider early forms of entertainment media and technology as conduits for involving museum audiences in the core content of educational material.

Before long he invited me to participate in my first planning/ conceptual charrette and our long and mutually satisfying association was under way. Over the next decade, I worked closely with Buzz, and his team on a wide variety of culturally oriented projects and came to consider him a close friend and confidante.

Neltje Jens Affair

What with numerous office transitions and file restructuring, I cannot pin-point exactly when in the late 1980s Buzz called me about a new potential project in the Netherlands. I remember thinking it sounded a bit off the wall, but it was after all his call, so when he said the client is willing to pay our time and expenses to present our credentials, I packed my bag and off we went.

Although I had flown into Schiphol Airport and spent several days in Amsterdam on a previous occasion, I had never before been to Zeeland, the nation's western-most province. I expect the same was true for Buzz, so between us we had no real notion of the nation's internal geography. After almost 10 hours in the air and no small amount of alcohol, we were grateful to the client for being on hand as promised to whisk us away to our hotel for a much-anticipated rest.

Alas however, that was not to be. The two hearty Dutchmen that greeted us beyond the baggage area excitedly recited our plan for the day. First a leisurely two-hour drive through Rotterdam, Den Hague and other points of interest on the coast, and then on to Zierikzee where the final section of the famous Dutch Delta Works, the "Oosterscheldering" was being erected. This long, undulating barrier protecting the nation's coastline from frequent ravages of the North Sea is among the most ingenious feats ever accomplished by Dutch engineering. Consequently, its culmination was a cause for celebration and as it would turn out, the underlying reason for our presence.

Although a strain on tired eyes and minds, the running descriptions accompanying our journey was interesting and held our attention. When finally reaching our perceived destination, we looked forward with even greater anticipation to the deferred rest we were certain to be the reward for our patience. Once again however, our expectation was proven optimistic. Now, at the edge of a small lagoon stood not a charming country inn, but a grey steel-spired structure rising from the water below. This, explained our appointed guide was a spare support tower, built within a man-made reservoir to test a number of watertight and stability details, before it and a companion tower were sunk in the nearby sea bottom as the final barrier span installed.

The tower architecture itself, while impressive, was however not the ultimate objective of our orientation. Oh no, it was the inner workings of this unique anchored support, that was intended to whet our appetite for the project discussions that would ensue over the next several days.

After exchanging a brief eye-roll, Buzz and I duly expressed our keen interest in that experience in the days to come. Ah, said our hosts, but we must do this right now, since the test unit was to be dismantled the very next day at first light...and such an opportunity would never again be available!

Now Buzz, not always the most patient human on the planet was faced with the choice of either submitting to this extraordinary assault on his mind and body or blowing the entire project and getting the hell back to Amsterdam. Perhaps it was lack of sleep, or perhaps empathy for me as a neophyte in themed attraction planning, but Buzz resignedly opted to remain silent. He would regret that departure from his natural cynicism almost immediately as we stepped inside the tower to be confronted by a sturdy maintenance ladder mounted to an inside wall. I can see us now in my mind's eye; hard-hatted and yellow slicker-wrapped, descending hand-over-hand through this 10-story high volume not daring to look down. After what seemed an eternity, we were finally able to plant our feet firmly on the concrete floor. No verbal communication between us was required to confirm our gratitude for being alive.

For the next half hour or so, we were introduced to a number of engineering details that were critical to the performance of the structure that made the overall system reliable under various oceanic extremes.

In due time, our tour of the floor completed, our beaming hosts finally observed that we must be tired by now and deserving of a well-earned rest. Buzz, who I might remind you was well into his 60s at the time, breathed a sigh of relief and looking about the cavernous floor area said, "Well, that was really interesting; which way to the elevator?" Our hosts chuckled at this witticism thinking this to be an example of Buzz' well-known humor and started back toward the ladder. Unthinkable as it may seem, our only way out was up the ladder! I suggested that Buzz precede me so I might watch for any missteps and perhaps deflect the endless expletives that he made no effort to disguise as we made the climb.

Once on terra firma we were this time rewarded with a very brief ride to our lodgings and finally settled in for a late dinner and a good night's sleep.

The next day, refreshed and but still unclear about why we were here in this fascinating land of windmills, dykes and canals, all was revealed. During our continuing orientation we learned that in the course of gaining control of the tidal forces that in the past had regularly overcome the system of earthen dykes protecting large dairy farms along the coast, the barrier in this final section had inadvertently created a new strip of dry land and captive lagoon. The newly formed island, named Neelte Jans, which we in turn explored with our hosts, also featured a fine sandy beach that quickly became a destination attraction for residents and visitors alike. The project contractors had also constructed a service building on the island in which a number of technical exhibits related to the barrier development had been installed.

It was in the interest of substantially increasing tourism to the Island that the local government was seeking professional assistance to optimize both the natural and built environment of the island. While many ideas for attracting tourists had been discussed internally for some time, the community leaders recognized the need for an attraction that would not only be unique enough to meet that objective but would prove economically sustainable for many years to come.

By the end of this second day of our visit, Buzz was weary of trying to understand the often heavily accented English of the local folks. We begged off dinner with the client that evening, ostensibly to prepare our presentation for the following day, but actually because Buzz had completely lost patience with the entire affair. Our reservations notwithstanding, we put our heads together that evening and sketched out a conceptual approach to meeting the goals expressed by our hosts.

The next morning, energized by our vision for the project and a good night's sleep, we were conveyed to our meeting venue by our hosts. At that penultimate moment, we learned for the first time that we were not the only consultant under consideration but one of two, and that we would be first on the schedule, with the second to follow that afternoon. I suppose we shouldn't have been surprised at this new information and it did take the wind out of our sails a bit, but Buzz resented the fact that they gave us so little advanced notice, adding to his already expressed angst.

To further compound this perceived breech of courtesy, we discovered at the last-minute that the Kodak carousel slide tray we requested well before leaving the states was made for European use and was a mismatch for our slide mounts. Nevertheless, we soldiered on, feeding our slides into the projector one at a time.

Buzz of course peppered his remarks with an assortment of witticisms and wisecracks that went completely over the heads of the audience of 30 or 40 local officials, while I wrestled with the hastily reshuffled images we selected in support of our conceptual recommendations.

In the end, our presentation was well received and stimulated a number of questions, which I fielded as I sensed that his attention suddenly seemed elsewhere.

After we wrapped up to sustained applause, our hosts told us privately that our competitor was an all-European team led by the well-known German architect Frie Otto and asked should the occasion arise, if we would be willing to collaborate with them. I assured them it would be a privilege.

Once back at our hotel an on our own, I asked Buzz why he seemed so detached during the Q&A. He looked at me with that incomparably impish grin and said, "I wasn't detached, I was just so tired of trying to understand those guys, that I wasn't wearing my hearing aids!"

Gotta love that man!

Before we left the next day, we were told by our hosts that when Frie Otto was asked the same final question after his presentation about a potential collaboration with us, he responded with a resounding, "Nein."

We didn't get the job.

Buzz's Name Kept Coming Up – It Changed my Life

BY Michael C. Mitchell

Planning a World's Fair in Alaska

I first entered into Buzz's life as his client. The State of Alaska was riding high after opening North America's largest oil field at Prudhoe Bay. Production began in 1977 when the Alaska Pipeline was completed. I was asked to serve as the Executive Director of their plan to utilize some of their new found wealth to hold a World's Fair to celebrate their 25th Anniversary of Statehood. After making inquiries as to who could best advise us on how to organize a World's Fair, one name kept coming up – Harrison "Buzz" Price. Upon contacting Buzz he brought his whole gang, including Disney Stalwarts like Bob Jani and Rich Battaglia, the manager of Seattle's 1960 World Fair, Ewen Dingwell, and of course the all-important Nick Winslow. It was then and there that I first experienced Buzz's famous charrette process.

Little did I know that this chance encounter would forever change my life. One might rightly ask how such a puckish personality could have such an outsized impact on ones destiny. Buzz dazzled, bewitched and confounded many with his brilliance, but for me, he presented a way of looking at the world that deeply resonated with my own desire to understand underlying structures. Although some might say it was his powerful analytics, his sense of numbers, but for me it was something different.

Buzz innately understood that people needed a way to size up the elephant in the room. He knew that some had grabbed the trunk and thought they understood what was needed while those with the tail had an entirely different map in their mind. His genius took two concepts, that of the charrette and more importantly, the use of numerical analysis to compare and contrast potential decisions, and turned them into useful and dynamic practical tools. I refer to it as sizing, though some would say proportion, others might say it was a way to get your hands around a project. However you viewed it, it was a profound and powerful way of looking at the world.

I grew up always being the best in my class with numbers. They were a comfort, easily manipulated in my head, a way to keep track of things. I received that gift from my mother who kept numerical lists of everything, from the cost of gas to the time it took to drive to our vacation home on Friday nights; numerical lists that were in fact in such abundance over 50 years that they were catalogued in boxes that filled her garage. What Buzz brilliantly did was bring order to all those numbers packed away in useless boxes. He gave us a mental structure, a way to organize the world. Moving the unknown into the knowable, the unseen into the concrete, a way to actually make sense of questions that always came up. How big should it be? How much should it cost? Can we make money? How many people will come?

The way Buzz thought about the world deeply impacted me, and many others that he touched as well. The tools he gave us have inspired those of us that fully understood their power to yield insights to the inexplicable, to carry on his work, crafting ever more powerful tools to 'size' a project, to bring order to confusion, to temper emotionally driven decisions with grounded facts.

1984 Los Angeles Olympics

When the oil prices collapsed in the early 1980s, and the State of Alaska abandoned their dream, Buzz worked his magic on my life once again by answering a request from Peter Ueberroth who was leading the 1984 Los Angeles Olympic Organizing Committee. Buzz was one of Peter's chief consultant's. Peter had asked Buzz if he could recommend anybody to take over the planning of the Games. Buzz called and explained the situation saying that he recommended me and that I should come to Los Angeles to meet with Peter.

Following Buzz's generous recommendation, Peter and I did meet and I was able to apply all that I had learned from Buzz as the Group Vice-President of Planning and Control (Finance) of the Games. The planning tools that Buzz had developed formed an important basis for the planning methodology I utilized for the Games. The Olympics also afforded me the fortunate opportunity to be near Buzz and remain an associate and friend for the remainder of his life.

I was honored to work with Buzz over a 25 year period. I always felt we were kindred spirits, perhaps simply because we were both born in Portland, Oregon (Buzz a few miles south in Oregon City), a place that fostered independent thinking, even a bit iconoclastic. He certainly possessed both those traits in spades. And any discussion about the great Buzz Price is wholly incomplete without a nod to Annie, who made all of what Buzz was, possible. My wife and I always deeply enjoyed visits to their home or ours, where discussions often turned to beauty, and art and music.

Buzz and Annie brought grace, and beauty and understanding and just a few answers to an uncertain world.

Five Decades with Buzz

BY Nick Winslow

I had the distinct pleasure and privilege of knowing Buzz for nearly five decades. Seems like a long time but it really wasn't. If anything, it all passed too quickly. We were, as he described it, "shirt-tail relatives," (his sister Pat was married to my uncle Wendell). That being said, our two branches of the family were not particularly close so I can't say Buzz and I knew much about each other early on. Being kin complicated the idea of going to work for him for all of about two minutes, after which we settled into decades where our relationship changed from employee to colleague/partner/confidant to client and, throughout all, dear friend. But I get ahead of myself. I will leave it to others to provide professional anecdotes. There are a ton of them. I want to talk about the person I knew for most of my life.

The Fifties

I first met Buzz sometime in the mid-'50s at a family gathering at their home on Irving Street in Hancock Park. The occasion stuck in my memory for two reasons. First, I was intrigued by the idea of someone having the name Buzz. It's the kind of name that sticks with you when you're a kid and, as I learned over time, was fitting to the person I came to know. The second reason I remember the day was what was sitting in the driveway. Buzz had a silver Mercedes 300 SL gull wing. It was the most beautiful and exotic automobile I had ever seen. It had custom luggage made to fit in the trunk. Truly a masterpiece of design and engineering. (I learned later that Buzz had received the 300SL as payment for a $5,500 consulting fee. I don't know when he sold it but it's too bad he did. They are currently worth over $1 million.) We didn't come in contact again for more than a decade and I did not follow what Buzz was doing professionally while I was in college and graduate school, but the image of the person and his very hot car stayed with me until we met again in the '60s.

The Sixties

I finished my MBA at Stanford in 1966 and then did a stint in the Air Force. Prior to going off to defend our country I had accepted a job as a brand manager with Colgate Palmolive in New York, but I was never enthused about either the job or the location. Seeing this unease, my mother suggested I go see our shirt-tail relative, Buzz Price. She had no idea what Buzz did but she knew he was successful and perhaps he would be interested in a young Stanford MBA, so I went to see him. Buzz explained what ERA was all about. It did feasibility studies focusing on theme parks and real estate developments (this was the era of the gigantic second home lot sale programs). He asked a few questions to see if I could reason and articulate my thoughts, introduced me to a couple of the VPs (the old pros in their early 30s) and offered me a job at about half my Colgate salary.

Growing up with the excitement of the opening of Disneyland made the choice a no-brainer. Theme parks vs. tooth paste. Manhattan Beach vs. Manhattan. SOLD. On my first day at ERA Buzz called me in to welcome me to the company, closed the door, and made it abundantly clear that shirt-tail relative or no, I had to carry my weight professionally or I would be gone. If anything, he would expect more from me. It scared the hell out of me but it was a good lesson about understanding the differences between personal and professional relationships.

The culture at ERA in the late '60s was eclectic and exciting, probably akin to some of the tech companies today. It had a small cadre of senior people who provided leadership and direction, but the vast majority of the 50-plus staff were young, smart, ambitious and, in many cases, single. Buzz drove us hard. We had to keep our billed time ratios very high and the schedules were sometimes relentless. Accordingly, most worked very long hours and on weekends. That led to a lot of staff fraternization and a certain amount of hanky-panky (hey, it was the '60s). I always believed Buzz had a keen understanding of the social dynamic of the place and had the managerial skill to rein things in before they got out of hand.

An important part of the social dynamic were three major parties each year—one commercial, one social and one philanthropic. ERA had a contract with the State of Kentucky to promote investment in the state. Every year, the leaders of Kentucky's business sector got a boondoggle trip to Southern California to meet potential investment partners.

The annual trip was capped by a lavish party at Buzz's home to which most of the ERA professional staff was invited. Buzz sent people scouring all of Los Angeles County to buy every bottle of Makers Mark they could find. It was the preferred whiskey of the Kentuckians but not readily available in LA at the time. The party was a boisterous affair that produced a lot of hangovers but I don't know about its success in stimulating the Kentucky economy. The second major event was the annual ERA Christmas party. Like most holiday parties of the era it featured lots of alcohol and lots of fraternization.

The third event, and I think the most interesting, was the annual Disney Artists for CalArts event (DAFCA). The event was a fundraiser at the Price home highlighting the fine art work of artists like Herb Ryman. We got to hob knob with some of the rich and famous, buy some very good art at reasonable prices, and know that we were supporting something very important to the Prices. Buzz made it clear that CalArts was an important legacy item to Walt Disney and it was something Walt asked Buzz to shepherd through to maturity. The DAFCA event was part of that effort and very dear to Anne and Buzz's heart.

I included this little commentary on the social life at ERA for three reasons;

1) Buzz created a culture at ERA that was like an extended family. Yes, we worked hard and put in long hours, but we were also welcomed into the Price home to meet their friends and associates as equals. Ultimately, this built confidence and social maturity that was important both personally and professionally.

2) The love between Buzz and Anne was pervasive in all our associations with them. They were different in many ways but totally connected, and while we might over-imbibe and over carouse inside and outside office hours, none of us would ever do anything that would embarrass us with Annie.

3) We all knew how important CalArts was to Buzz and that he presided over some very trying times at the institution. His steadfastness and leadership were examples of giving back to the community that rubbed off on all of us.

The Seventies

I started the 1970s working on ERA's geographic expansion, with stints at offices in Washington, DC, Florida and San Francisco. We were growing rapidly and found it advantageous to be closer to some of our key clients and markets. It also meant project management was more complicated because the branch offices often utilized the services of pros from the home office in LA. Coordinating proposal efforts also became complicated. Occasionally, two separate offices of ERA would bid in competition with each other for the same job. Buzz, of course, was the person who had to hold all this together. He did so by early, and I mean VERY early, phone calls. Despite the three hour time difference, I was always at my desk by 8 a.m. because the inevitable, terse and pungent call from Buzz would inevitably provide a stimulating start to my day.

I want to add one anecdote from this period because it is so unique. Buzz was visiting Washington DC and we were holding a staff dinner at my apartment in his honor. Not surprisingly, there was a lot of alcohol. Toward the end of the evening Buzz sidled up to me and said something to the effect, "Nick, I'll be back in Washington next week and in the meantime, I would like you to buy me a 1,000 cc Honda motorcycle. I don't care what Annie says, I have two weeks of accrued vacation time coming and I want to drive that SOB across the country. Oh yes, and get me a helmet with "The Green Weenie" stenciled on it." The next day as he was driving to the airport, he said to Daryl Butcher, my partner in crime in Washington, "For heaven's sake, don't let Winslow buy that motorcycle!"

By the way, Buzz loved to drive fast. Perhaps it was a lingering affection for the long gone 300SL. In any event, several members of the ERA staff recounted fearsome stories of road trips with Buzz. Buzz driving through the Rockies, careening through curves with one hand

Nick Winslow & Buzz Price at IAAPA Expo, Orlando, Florida

HP Charrette for Queen Emma Foundation at Foundation Office in the early '80s.
Left to right, unidentified, John Carl Warnecke, Nick Winslow, Buzz Price and Ray Watson

on the wheel and the other on a chicken leg. Buzz setting a new land speed record driving from downtown LA to Palm Springs so he wouldn't be late for a presentation. As far as I know his affection for driving fast never got him into serious trouble but it sure scared that hell out of some of his passengers.

In 1969, Buzz sold ERA to Planning Research Corporation (PRC), a conglomerate of professional service firms that was listed on the NYSE. It was a way for the founders of companies with no significant assets other than their people to cash out. PRC argued that the synergy that would exist between these prestigious and talented companies would stimulate growth and everyone would get rich. It didn't happen for a number of reasons, and Buzz led a revolt against the founding management, ultimately ending up as the new chairman. By this time I had left and gone to work for Paramount Pictures, but Buzz and I stayed in contact. Things didn't improve – the concept behind PRC was flawed – and Buzz was ultimately ousted by many of the same people who originally supported him.

He and Annie were living in an apartment at the Watergate in DC at the time and I stopped by for dinner one night while I was in town. Buzz wasn't despondent over his ouster – he clearly understood what had happened to him, although he was not at all happy about it – but he was at sea regarding what he would do next. Being the head of a NYSE listed company had been heady stuff, a hard act to follow.

After dinner, with Annie retired, we began a talk that lasted nearly all night about career strategies, options, personal goals, etc. Buzz had tentatively been offered the top job at a health care company in Houston and was wondering whether or not to take it. I opined that despite the fact that he was one of the smartest people I knew, he didn't know anything about health care and had no support base in Houston. I thought it was a very high risk opportunity that could end badly. We also discussed the merits of going back to LA where he was established, and returning to a business where he was a dominant force, doing feasibility consulting in the recreation field. I don't know how much our conversation that night influenced him but the next time I saw Buzz he had hung out his shingle under the banner of Harrison Price Company (HPC) and was carving out a new chapter in his legendary career.

The Eighties

By 1982, Buzz was gaining traction with HPC and I was miserable running a failing video post-production house in Hollywood. One day Buzz called and wanted to know if I would be interested in joining him and some other industry pros for an inter-disciplinary storyboard

TEA's "Mr. Mission Control" - Harrison "Buzz" Price -
at the original Mission Control, Johnson Space Center, circa 1987

conference focused on development opportunities for a cinema site in Honolulu. He called this a charrette, a term he had picked up from his architect son David. The idea of being paid for a few days of consulting in Hawaii sounded very attractive so I agreed to participate.

We had a great time, the sessions were fun and interesting, and the client was thrilled with the outcome. While in Honolulu I mentioned to Buzz that I was not happy at United Video and he began pitching me on coming over to HPC. It was an easy sell and the rest, as they say, is history. We worked together for the next decade, building HPC into a force in the recreation and real estate feasibility fields, honing the charrette into an established format that our clients came to appreciate. We did not attempt to build a firm as big as ERA had been, but to have a group of seasoned pros who could each hold their own in highly demanding projects. The concept worked and HPC developed a terrific reputation and a loyal client base.

Buzz loved the English language. I suspect he developed this love from Annie since I doubt it came from his engineering studies at CalTech. Regardless of source or motivation, his skills were extraordinary. Buzz's reports were a pleasure to read and his conversation always scintillating. It is not surprising, then, that Buzz and Annie became close with Marty and Leah Sklar, world class wordsmiths in their own rights. (Marty headed up Walt Disney Imagineering and had first caught the attention of Walt Disney as a fledgling journalist). Both the Prices and the Sklars had second homes in Palm Springs, and one weekend they invited me to join them for brunch. When we arrived these two formidable couples were engaged in a competitive word game involving spontaneously composed limericks based on absurd topics. The final round consisted of a delightful ditty dealing with necrophilia. The banter was brilliant, witty, pungent and a delight.

In 1988, tragedy struck. My son died suddenly and unexpectedly of heart disease. Buzz was the first person at the hospital. He had lost his oldest son in a tragic accident in the early '50s and understood more than anyone what I was feeling and about to go through. His support helped me through this painful period and I will be forever grateful for his friendship and counsel at this time.

The Nineties

By the early '90s Buzz was still running HPC but I had moved over to Warner Bros. to head up its fledgling international theme park division. My charge was to expand the WB park footprint around the globe, patterning new attractions after our highly successful Movie World park in Australia. In a major role shift I called on Buzz to conduct a feasibility study for a park we were considering in Spain. In his book "Walt's Revolution! By the Numbers," Buzz includes this study in his list of 16 favorite assignments. As Buzz noted in his recap, "The question was whether the old man could still play chess." My answer was a resounding YES. The study was vintage Buzz – terrific data, cogent analysis and brilliantly written. It was a delight to work with Buzz on this project, our last collaboration but one of the best.

The New Millennium

By the time the new millennium came around both Buzz and I were largely retired although we each did some consulting work. He and Annie were living in Palm Springs so I didn't see too much of them. Ultimately, they moved to the Mt. San Antonio Gardens in Claremont, where I was on the board, so I had the chance to catch up with them from time to time. Somewhat but not completely surprising, Buzz developed an interest in poetry while at "The Gardens." I suspect it was his way of "keeping the juices flowing."

I believe there was a sense of poetry about the end of his life. Buzz's health had been declining in 2009 when he was asked by the Disney family to speak at the opening of The Walt Disney Family Museum in San Francisco. By all accounts his talk was fabulous – very much vintage Buzz. It was his last hurrah. A few months later he was gone.

There was only one Buzz Price. I will always remember him for his intelligence and wit, passion for the things important to him and most of all Annie, compulsive list making, integrity, impatience, energy, leadership skills, concern for others, devotion to his family, sense of humor, love of language and a friendship that lasted through all the ups and downs of our lives. It was a great ride.

CHAPTER 11

A Buzz Story from Buzz

BY "Buzz" Price

Lead Kindly Light

Through the years, dad sent me copies of many of his speeches and as I researched this book, I found this one and found it to be as relevant today as it was when he wrote it.

Buzz was addressing the PRC Presidents Council comprised of Division Heads, in Montreal, Canada on June 30, 1974. I was a student at the Graduate School of Design at Harvard University and living in Cambridge at the time. The speech, "Lead Kindly Light," provides us with a Guideline for Contemporary Ethical Business Practices. I did not edit or correct. It's true, vintage Buzz!

Buzz during the PRC era

One way to start this discussion is to ask you all to please turn your hymnals to page 492. We will rise and sing on verse of the old hymn – "Lead kindly light amid the encircling graft."

For the first time I understand that the preacher has a tough job. I've been stewing on this assignment for days. I've wondered should a man who went to see Behind the Green door be leading this discussion? It's not easy to give out advice to a bunch of cagey pros in a very personal area of operation. The subject is on the agenda because we were advised not so long ago that we had a flat-out case of payola in one of the companies and we were asked how to handle it. In the process of figuring out what to do – getting a legal opinion and other research we got the idea that the subject was indeed complex – not simply black and white – requiring adroit and prudent judgements – so Bill Hodson asked me to put the subject out on the table here at this meeting.

Anyway, I've been doing my homework. I've read the Gospel According to Peanuts and the New Morality by Bishop Pike. I have come to the conclusion that it is indeed appropriate for a public company like PRC – particularly one selling professional services – in the particular time of history in which a Vice President of the United States was disbarred and removed from office – for elementary payola to talk out loud about a subject which is only reluctantly talked about – namely, what are the essential ethical parameters – the practical limits which should be implemented by the companies of PRC which submit maybe 8,000 proposals a year and book a quarter of them.

For it would be a shame for a wrong approach on one of these 8,000 proposals to jeopardize the total effort – as to reputation and ability to do business. And we have had a near miss or two or three in our companies over the years. So, I will try to define some tests that apply to the small number of situations we are really focusing on – the conflict of interest situations – the bagman payola area which most of us have had to deal with at some time – a little or a lot.

In this discussion I will use several words which need definition:

> **Payola** – a euphemism for a payoff, usually in money or perquisite, given to influence a decision maker.

> **Bribery** – the legal term for payola or a payoff.

> **Finder's Fee** – an emolument paid to a person or persons providing the brokerage service of putting people together to do business.

  The line drawn between payola and finder's fee is an important one.

> **Bagman** – one who delivers money or payola to a decision maker.

  This word is often carelessly applied to finder's situations which muddies up the line drawing process.

> **Hanky Panky** – an uncertainly suspicious business or social practice.

Propensity for payola varies in the companies as to whether it's a little or a lot because of the action of several variables which effect ways of doing business – the mores of the trade.

> **The first variable is geography –**

Maine and Montana are different than Maryland
and Mississippi.
Brazil is different than Canada.
England is different than France.

> **A second variable is standard of living –**

Payoffs may be more standard in a poor country – morality
becomes a luxury for some.

> **A third variable is the nature of the urban environment –**

Is Chicago "crookerder" than Salem, Oregon?
Is New York greedier than Rochester?

> **A fourth variable is the nature of the customer -**

The Feds tend to be generally cleaner than some state and
local jurisdictions.
The FBI is less fractious than the Texas Railroad Commission.
Defense is more circumspect than regulatory bodies generally,
I suspect.
Consumer oriented situations (Madison Avenue) have been more
scandalized than machinery manufacturers.

> **A fifth variable is the differences in types of professional service –**

The "mordita" (the Spanish word for bite) comes more often in
the big money areas of engineering and contracting than it
does in management consulting.

> **A sixth variable is the difference in governments –**

Political leaders on the take can hardly police commercial practice.
Another way to say it is that the mordita is less risky the higher it
is located on the chain of command.
If the King of Grainola's son-in-law is a non-working joint venturer
on your contract – you are not likely to get in trouble in
Grainola – unless the King is deposed.

> **A seventh influence is local legal tradition –**

The English civil service born of the English common law
traditionally has been famously clean.
New York has tougher laws than Alabama or New Jersey.

So, some of you will never run into the problem – some of you will
hit it often. At little ERA to my knowledge we were hit up for payola –
money for the decision maker – 4 or 5 times out of 4,000 plus jobs.
Maybe 20 to 30 times we had to deal with finders of diverse kinds of

which a couple might have been suspect as to their relationship in the decision-making process.

Let me talk for a moment about our research on this subject. With no difficulty we found quantities of material on business ethics – mostly recent – in our 18th floor library. It is an active topic today with most managements. The present temper of business according to this stack of material – and it sounds part real and part public relations – is that we must do good deeds in a list a yard long – we must be concerned about basic problems in education, environmental clean-up, race relations, job enrichment, public health, transportation problems, political participation, corrective urban planning, geriatrics, the quality of life, etc. The articles call for business to lead the way in these fields – that it must do so to offset its low credibility as measured by a variety of polls and special studies – some of this was touched on in San Diego at the long range planning meeting.

Only a few articles in Business Week and the Harvard Business Review dealt directly with the conflict of interest and business practices area. But nevertheless, I get the idea that this new preoccupation with the need for high standards is for real – in its impact on how we will be doing business in this country. There is a massive intolerance of the Spiro Syndrome and the feeling one gets is that the "new morality" is here to stay for our time. In our prior years we have had threatened exposure of conflict of interest which would be worse to deal with today.

Some of you – in this stringent atmosphere – today or tomorrow will be pondering how best to handle a piece of business in which there is a flavor of pay-off. How have our societies and institutions dealt with the situation before? How do we develop a list of do's and don'ts? Theology and history are full of relevant slogans for putting on the wall – from caveat emptor to the Golden Rule in all its many versions. The problem with the Golden Rule is the ambiguity surrounding the words "do unto others".

Nearly a hundred years ago the Rotarians devised a code called The Four Way Test

> Is it the Truth?
> Is it fair to all concerned?
> Will it build goodwill and friendship?
> Will it be beneficial to all concerned?

The problem with that is that you can build a good case for bribing the Pope if the result is socially constructive.

An early American test – "Would you do it if you were President of the United States?" is no longer considered foolproof.

In developing my own list, I debated long on whether to define constraints – what not to do – or guides –what to do. Too much material on ethics is negative simplistically thou shall not. Positive guidelines are more complex. Unable to make up my mind I have done both.

The list of do's is an acronym so you can remember it. It's a five-point list that spells the word STALL.

1. S is for Sleep. If the deal keeps you awake at night you better examine it. Consult your friendly group vice president. I learned this one from experience.

2. T is for Television. If the arrangement gets to be public can you defend it on television with your family watching? That's from Arjay Miller.

3. A is for Advice. When in doubt get advice before you do it. See your lawyer or our lawyer Ken Poovey. That's from Ken Poovey.

4. L is for Legality. Is it legal in the local situation and jurisdiction involved? Walter Rauscher, Senior Vice President of American Airlines and a well-regarded Group Vice President of Whitaker went to jail under the Commercial Bribery Statute of New York State for condoning kickbacks made to their subordinates by vendors.

5. L is for the Los Angeles Times. My founding partner of ERA Herb Holley said more than once to me on occasions of this nature – How will it look on the front page of the Los Angeles Times?

My list of don'ts is short and sweet, and probably not long enough.

1. Don't deal in cash (don't carry a bag.)

2. Don't transmit company checks or other fancy emoluments to a party participating in decision making processes in a buying situation.

3. If you suspect hanky panky is wanted by a buyer don't proceed without insulation from the situation by a third party like a prime contractor, a joint venturer, a lawyer, a PR man – someone who can function as a finder – an explainable service.

4. Beware of finders who must remain quiet and confidential.

5. Don't confuse a kickback with a finder's fee – know the difference.

6. If you know there is dirty work afoot – don't proceed without legal advice. There is a whole different set of rules when you know there is hanky panky as opposed to merely suspecting that there is.

I have tried to spell out some guidelines of procedure but let me emphasize that instinct is not to be underestimated in dealing with these problems. I think you must be able to smell trouble. Whatever the guidelines you must have some flexibility in dealing with the environment or give up doing business with the King of Grainola.

Nevertheless, I recommend that we be shrewd and prudent in the assumption of risk. Today we must do more than practice the 11th commandment (thou shall not get caught). We must be willing and able to pass up tainted business unless there is a way to clean it up and the process of cleaning it up is an art form which is now open for discussion.

But first I would like to read a quatrain composed especially for this occasion this morning.

> Said the circumspect King of Grainola
> Who suspected a deal was payola
> There will be no such chicanery
> in my royal grainery,
> Cause I can't tell shit from shinola.

> His son-in-law promptly retorted
> Don't worry I have this thing sorted
> I have all the money and none of its funny
> And no one will know it's extorted.

> The transaction was made in Hong Kong
> Where bribery couldn't be wrong
> They were careful to launder it
> But the Feds were soon on to it
> Now in Sing-Sing they're singing their song.

Buzz, a numbers guy that loved language, provides guidelines for contemporary ethical business practice that ring equally true for today. Human nature as it is, suggests that sometimes only the names change while the story remains the same. Thank you dad.

CHAPTER 12

"Buzz" Stories from Home & Beyond

BY David A. Price AIA

How Lucky We Were

Buzz was our leader, mentor and colleague during the HPC years. I'm grateful for the home base head start I had as a son. I shared day one with my twin sister Dana, a talented artist living with her husband Ken in Sausalito, California. My brother Bret, a very successful sculptor in Orange County, California was born a year later. My younger sister Holly, the last to follow, is a retired professional singer with the Los Angeles Master Chorale and taught voice at Pomona College. Our older brother Steve (three years my senior) was also part of our den but died in a childhood accident at the age of nine.

We were all lucky to have had two Type-A parents in our lives both of whom lived to the age of 89. My siblings and I were encouraged to be creative, work hard and chase our dreams by two parents that loved each other through the highs and lows of a remarkable life they shared.

What comes to mind is how mom and dad encouraged us as children to learn how to express ourselves. Writing, music, making things and the arts struck a chord with all my siblings. While we went to public schools for the most part, in a sense we were also homeschooled when it came to encouragement and support. What speaks to me so clearly today was how lucky we all were. Memories endure.

Second Floor Garage Office

In 1953, we were a young family living in a neighborhood with lots of kids in the heart of Los Angeles, the Larchmont District. Our home had a special bonus feature, a three-car garage with a second floor that became Dad's home office and sanctuary for Dad's slide ruler and wall mounted Mylar covered maps. The garage office was where Dad studied site location options and fine-tuned planning and metric calculations for Disneyland. It was the initial home office for the company he founded – Economic Research Associates (ERA).

Next to Dad's office was an all-purpose kid's room that housed an assorted collection of stamps, coins, a train set and rocks. It was a convenient way for Dad to keep an eye on us while he worked and my first introduction to market research through the eyes of a child. Dad's desk was a massive laminated door that had a wide drawer mounted under the desk top for pencils, erasers, paper clips and pens. I loved sorting through the drawer and sharpening pencils. When ERA set up office in downtown LA, there were more drawers of pencils to look after and opportunities to draw.

Best Wishes to Buzz from Walt, © Disney

Christmas Gifts from Walt

Every Christmas through the '50s the Price family received a large box from Walt Disney filled with individually wrapped gifts. Growing up, Walt Disney and Christmas were bound together. Had the gifts remained unopened in their original packaging, we would have a collector's trove today, but as children we had no such thoughts. On Christmas morning, gifts and wrappings were scattered across the living room floor and beyond with only family memories remaining.

What continues today across a multi-cultural themed entertainment landscape is the blending of holiday celebrations and seasons throughout the year that takes place at all Disney Parks as well as other major theme park attractions worldwide. Our large box containing gifts from Walt Disney at Christmas quickly ushered in an era of retail invention that filled the imaginations of children everywhere.

Picking up Dad & Walt at the Airport

Well before LA's airport officially became LAX, I remember my siblings and me piling into the family station wagon with Mom and driving across LA's surface streets to pick up Dad at the airport who was returning from a business trip with Walt Disney. Security was also different back then, you could greet arrivals at the gate. Dad and Walt walked through the gate. Walt was holding the hand of a little black girl as we walked together to the baggage claim area. Being at the airport was exciting and Dad was returning home. The crowd around us was very excited to see Walt Disney.

I've not forgotten the memory of the little girl holding Walt's hand and how caring and attentive he was to her. He seemed like a very friendly man that was kind to children. I wonder who the little girl was and if she remembers as I do? Since then, how many children have since walked down Main Street or sat on a bench holding the hand of their favorite Disney character at Disneyland? "That's a number that can be crunched," as Dad would say. Dad would also understand the uncalculatable – the value of someone taking the time to hold your hand. Sometimes the smallest things are the biggest.

Neighborhood Fun Zone

Building your own neighborhood fun zone happened fast when you're just a kid. My childhood friend Arden Day lived at the end of the block giving us a corner street location for food and beverage (cookies and lemonade) and a lawn area for attractions (miniature golf, horseshoes and board games). We lived in a neighborhood full of kids meaning the market area was well defined and market demand was positive. We weren't too concerned about our return on investment as long as the lemonade and backup Kool-Aid was in supply and we were having fun. I think we were acting out what we saw in our young world and taking control as far as our imaginations would take us. There's a saying, "Find what you like doing as a child and do it as an adult." Some are lucky enough to do that.

Our fun zone eventually expanded to the corner across the street. It was at the base of a pretty substantial hill (it seemed so at the time). The sidewalk running down the hill made a 90-degree turn at the base with not much of a landing zone. It was perfect for a new challenge and the advent for something we called skateboarding. Our skateboards were made of 2x4's, 24-inches in length with wheels fashioned from old metal-skates that had been repurposed and attached to the underside with a myriad assemblage of screws and nails.

We were too young to tap into the enterprising opportunities that awaited but others would and in time skateboard culture and the X-Games were born. The economic impacts are measurable. The world of skateboarding has been fully embraced by corporations and retail. Companies like Iconix seized upon it. Sponsors jumped in. As in most cases, there are winners and losers. But for us kids back in the day, we were all winners as long as we made the turn at the base of the hill!

Painting and Drawing

What luck to have parents that encouraged me to follow my interest in drawing! It led me to sign up for pre-college studies in painting and drawing at Chouinard Art School in 1964 and 1965 for two 12-week sessions at three hours per week. Other high school kids like me were attending the pre-college studios and together we learned the fundamentals of drawing and painting by professional art instructors. The live studio drawing classes were entirely new to me. On another occasion we visited Bunker Hill to sketch Victorian homes that would in time disappear and become concert halls and museums. I loved it.

Chouinard had been acquired by CalArts (California Institute of Arts) and big plans were in the works. Following Walt Disney's death in 1966, the Disney family and other benefactors had pressed ahead to bring his cherished vision to fruition. "CalArts is the principal thing I hope to leave when I move on to greener pastures," Walt had said. "If I can help provide a place to develop the talent of the future, I think I will have accomplished something."

By 1968, construction of the new CalArts campus began in Valencia. The centerpiece of the campus was a five-level, 500,000-square-foot mega-building designed by architects Ladd & Kelsey. While it wasn't in my plans at the time, by 1969 I had a summer job working for Thornton Ladd and John Kelsey located in Pasadena, California. Ten years later I would join Ladd, Kelsey & Woodard in Newport Beach, California and become vice president.

Back to being a 15 and 16 year old at Chouinard Art School. At the time I hadn't realized how special it was to have such encouraging parents. It was just my reality. It included drawing live nude models on Saturdays! In truth it was all business for me and my other talented artist friends. I also started creating a portfolio which would come in handy applying to colleges two years later.

As it turned out, the experience I had at Chouinard turned out to be a pretty good model for how to teach arts education to talented high school students. You put them in a college environment with other talented high school students, give them professional instruction and guidance and then "let the grass grow." That's exactly what Mom and Dad along with fellow founders of Ryman Arts had in mind when they created the program in 1990 after Herbert Ryman's passing.

Herbert Ryman (1910–1989) encouraged young artists throughout his long career as an artist, designer and Imagineer at Walt Disney Studios. After his death, his friends and family established Ryman Arts to carry on his philosophy and commitment to teach and encourage young artists to reach their full potential. The founders of Ryman Arts were Marty and Leah Sklar, Sharon Disney Lund, Lucille Ryman Carroll and my parents Anne and Buzz Price.

Over the past 28 years, Ryman Arts has engaged more than 6,000 Southern California teens in its core program and provided outreach activities to more than 20,000 inner city students. Almost all graduates go on to higher education, many alumni work in the creative industries, and all are poised for personal success.

This vibrant community of culturally diverse teens comes from more than 150 zip codes across five counties in Southern California. More than 80% live in low-income neighborhoods where schools provide little access to art and dropout rates are high.

I love and admire both my parents for having given me the opportunity to attend Chouinard's pre-college studies in painting and drawing and as it turned out, for not being satisfied with opening that door just for me. They and fellow founders of Ryman Arts opened up similar opportunities for countless other talented students. Today I'm

Ryman Arts Summer Garden Party - Phil Hettema, Board President; Diane Brigham, Executive Director; Host Tania Norris, Ryman Supporter; and David Price, Board Vice-President

Ryman Student, Maverick Mudge ('17)

Ryman Arts Studio Instruction

Ryman Student, Eloise Kabbaz Szabo ('16), Advanced Painting Class

very proud and honored to follow in their footsteps as a Ryman Arts Board Member. You can learn more about Ryman Arts by visiting its web site at RymanArts.org.

Bicycle Shop

I asked Dad once what Walt's key to success was. He said that Walt could take an old idea and make it better. Walt Disney said it well. "We don't invent, we just do better than we did before." The story of the bicycle offers a good example of how transformation often emanates from an old idea.

The first bicycle prototype was invented by Baron Karl von Drais in 1817 in Mannheim, Germany. Since then many efforts have been made to improve upon the original idea. As a young teen I had set up my own bike shop. I enjoyed taking bikes apart down to the frame for deep cleaning, painting, restoration and reassembling them like new as I had with my 15-gear Schwinn and others. In other garages and machine shops a revolution was unfolding in fabrication, manufacturing, distribution, marketing and sports recreation that would transform the culture and lifestyle of cycling worldwide. That transformation continues as we enter another wave of high tech cycles as part of a new strategy for building smart communities and cities.

The reinvention of the bicycle – taking an old idea and making it work better – demonstrates Walt's belief. Walt knew that he could create better family entertainment experiences than what was offered at the carnivals and fun zone attractions of the past. He and generations of talented Imagineers blazed a trail of continuous reinvention that created entirely new models for family entertainment across multiple platforms: television, film and media, theme parks and resorts, spectacle events and live performances, toys and games and other avenues that continue. It often started with taking an old idea and turning it into something better.

Keep It Simple

Dad taught me that if there's a simpler way of saying something, use it. He was also really a master at getting to the point especially at the right moment. In high school I learned about the architecture of Mies Van Der Rohe and the maxim "less is more." While I never latched onto rules with absolute devotion (some are meant to be broken), clarity of mind and thought seemed to have value particularly when it came to completing an assignment on time.

1 + 1 = 3

Dad allowed me to see math as a game. The key was conquering your fear and a willingness to practice. It got me as far as second year calculus in college. Dad would say that if you knew how to add, subtract, divide and multiply, you had the basic tool kit to get started in life. It also was at the core of his feasibility work. It helped me become an architect.

Over the family dinner table Dad could break down various kinds of human behavior by extolling the numbers. It led to some funny conversations. There wasn't a subject that couldn't be broken down by the numbers in some manner. Not all of it was useful research.

As an architect and designer, I learned that simple math isn't always what it seems especially among creatives. Sometimes 1 + 1 = 3! Dave & Buster's is a case in point. It started as two adjacent businesses – a pool hall and a restaurant. As the story goes, the owners decided to open the wall between the two uses and the resulting enterprise proved to be far greater than the sum of its parts. Dave & Buster's became a highly successful restaurant business located across the country in urban entertainment areas where patrons could eat and drink, play games and watch sports. There are other examples too: Great Wolf Lodge (hotel + water park = new paradigm); and Boomer's (arcade + outdoor rides & games = family attraction). The same math applies to soul mates.

Mineral King – Summer of '68

Walt Disney had hoped to build a summer and winter alpine resort located northeast of Visalia in the high mountains, south of Yosemite and Sequoia National Park in Mineral King. Walt's death in 1966 scuttled the project. Having been raised in a family of skiers, the news was disappointing. At the same time, I understood and appreciated the majesty of Mineral King. Our family along with two other families owned an old miner's cabin located in the heart of Mineral King Valley that had been built years ago around

Sam Gennawey, moderator, and panelists David Price & Ron Miller, Walt's son-in-law at The Walt Disney Family Museum, Sept. 9, 2012, discussing "Mineral King – Walt Disney's Last Lost Project"

Mineral King Site Visit, 1964 – Buzz Price, Ron Miller, Willie Scheffler, Walt Disney, John Kelsey and Bob Hicks

An artist's rendering of the proposed Mineral King resort, Master Plan Architects – Ladd Kelsey Architects, Pasadena, CA

the base of a giant Sequoia. That's right! We had a giant tree in the middle of a funky old cabin. During the summer of 1968, I spent weeks hiking and fishing in nearby creeks, reading and sketching, and repairing cabin walls and decking – all of which nourished my spirit before returning to college. A year later during the summer of '69, I was working at Ladd Kelsey Architects, the same firm that had prepared the Mineral King Ski Resort master plan. Walt Disney's last lost project had come to an end following his passing in 1966.

Mineral King is now part of our National Parks system, all of which is fully protected but the question remains for how long?

Ever since Yellowstone became the first national park in the history of the world on March 1, 1872, the ultimate conflict has been between use and preservation. Without visitors, the public's sense of ownership will fade, and the parks will be threatened. Without preservation, the destination will not be worth visiting. It has not always been this way. When the Northern Pacific Railroad reached the gateway to Yellowstone in 1883, travel within the park was restricted to all but the heartiest tourist and most guests participated in a five-day "grand tour."

In the 1920s, National Parks director Stephen Mather was an advocate for auto-camping and the outcome boomed in leisure travel

Urbino, Italy – David Price, Ink Sketch 1973 – David Price, Ink Sketch 1973

by automobile. We now expect to drive everywhere, and in the end, our National Parks are being loved to death.

In later years Dad and I talked about the irony of Walt's vision for Mineral King not coming to fruition. Walt had plans to limit the number of cars that would have been allowed into the valley by providing new rail service that would carry guests directly to the Alpine Village. Walt would have likely created a new paradigm of "Managed Tourism" and a model that could have been tested and adopted to meet the needs of today's Save the Parks challenge. The key is finding the right balance between meeting the needs of the public while protecting the very thing that drew them there in the first place.

The Wayward Wanderer & Buzz

In the summer of 1972 I took a one-year leave of absence from GSD at Harvard and headed to Europe on a Thomas J. Watson Fellowship for a year of reading, drawing and study, wandering through the cities, towns and villages of Europe as an aspiring young architect. My travels took me though France, Spain, Morocco, Italy, Switzerland, Austria and Germany.

Urbino, Italy – David Price, Ink Sketch 1973

Florence, Italy – David Price, Ink Sketch 1973

Perugia, Italy – David Price, Ink Sketch 1973

Palazzo Dei Papi, Orvieto, Italy – David Price, Ink Sketch 1973

Midway through the year I visited Salzburg for several days to meet with other Watson Fellows and afterwards met Dad in Munich arriving by train and checking into a 5-star hotel ahead of his arrival. My hair was down to my shoulders and I was traveling light. I had bought a white dinner coat at a flea-market so I would have something formal to wear at the hotel. I looked the part of a traveling wonderer. The hotel was posh as was our suite and I waited and then waited some more. I figured if Dad didn't show up, I had one hell of a hotel tab.

In time Dad arrived having been delayed in Moscow where he had spent several long days as the PRC front man meeting with the Chief Architect of Moscow. Dad said that this guy had more than 3,500 architects working for him. Dad too was moving up the ranks at PRC. He eventually became PRC's Chairman of the Board, a company ranked at the time as one of the largest A/E consulting firms in the United States. Looking back, Dad was often airborne heading to and fro, would soon relocate to Washington DC with Mom, living at the Watergate before eventually heading back to LA to launch Harrison Price Company (HPC). When I met Dad in Munich, I was moving through Europe on a Fellowship at my own rate of speed with plans to complete my Master's Degree at GSD in Cambridge upon my return. How good can it get!

Later that evening we headed out for dinner – father and son hitting the town to catch up. He had plenty of questions (and probably some he

Ranchamp Chapel, Haute-Saone, France – David Price, Ink Sketch 1973

Sainte-Maria de La Tourette, France – David Price, Ink Sketch 1973

Le Mont-Sant-Michel, Normandy, France – David Price, Ink Sketch 1973

didn't ask). I was the young man with a healthy dose of swagger some earned, some yet to be tested. It turned into a very full evening of laughter and conversation and the next morning we headed out in different directions. I would swing back through Los Angeles and the home front later that summer on my way back to GSD, but not before spending several more months dropping down into the "boot" of Italy. Pelican ink had become my companion and medium as I journeyed through the hilltop villages of Italy taking me as far south as Rome before heading home through France. My sketch pad was my passport all the way back to Luxembourg International. The year had filled my pores with enough creative juice to last a lifetime along with memories of my Dad and me in Munich.

Palm Springs – Rising Phoenix

After finishing graduate work in Boston and a couple of years working in Bean City, I returned home married with a son. I went to work for the Luckman Partnership, one of the Big Six architectural firms in Los Angeles, and later for Ladd Kelsey Woodard (LKW) in Newport Beach, California. Thornton Ladd and John Kelsey had been the master plan architects for Disney's short lived Mineral King project in addition to Cal/Arts in Valencia and the Norton Simon Museum in Pasadena. LKW closed in late 1980 and shortly thereafter I opened my own firm in Orange County, California under my own name.

I was very fortunate to have two projects at the start: the KMST television station in Monterey, California for Retlaw Enterprises and a second home for my parents in Palm Springs, California. The original home had burned to the ground when house painters working inside accidently sparked a fire. Nobody was injured but the home was destroyed.

The Palm Springs house eventually became home base for family gatherings and a place for Mom and Dad to reboot and relax. The downstairs office was later added and is where Dad's book, "Walt's Revolution! By the Numbers" was largely written.

Designing a house for my parents was a journey and a process fueled by the intimacy, love, respect and mystery of family dynamics. It was emotionally draining at times, very creative and led to the pouring of wine on a few occasions to rally ourselves. In a few instances when Mom and Dad had diametrically opposed views or I was clinging to a young architect's conviction, the master of the HPC charrette would turn to me and say, "figure it out," or words to that effect.

The home became a relaxing sanctuary from which my talented siblings and I found opportunities to share our artistic talents: Bret's many sculptures and ceramic works, Dana's tapestries and artworks,

Residence of Anne & Buzz Price, Palm Springs, CA American Institute of Architects, Orange County Chapter Residential Design Award, Architect – David A. Price AIA

Holly's classical voice ringing through the spaces and of course for myself as architect. In the end, the home received a Design Award from the AIA Orange County chapter and local recognition in a town known for its beautiful desert lifestyle and architecture.

On many occasion, sometimes with family gatherings drawing to a close, Dad would be packed and departing for the Palm Springs Airport in route to a scheduled HPC charrette.

Charrette – French for Cart

I was a second year architecture graduate student at Harvard University, Graduate School of Design. Dad called and mentioned that he was conducting "inter-disciplinary" workshops at work. I mentioned how design charrettes were an intense sometimes overnight part of the learning experience at GSD. He wanted to know about the term "charrette" and I mentioned that it was a French word for "cart" used by architectural students at École des Beaux Arts to cart around their drawings and supplies. I further explained how these same carts were used to carry around the guillotined heads of the unfortunate during the French Revolution. I didn't realize then that other charrette purposes lay ahead. But a seed had been planted in Dad's fertile mind.

David Price, Aspen Institute Conference,
Aspen, CO, 1974

Ten years later I was being pulled into the HPC charrettes process, meeting talented colleagues and jumping into blue-sky deliberations. Buzz was the captain and we were the crew. Destination to be determined in flight.

Since Dad's charrettes involved a pre-selected group of highly skilled and creative strategist, the need to decapitate was deemed extreme and never necessary. On a few occasions an uncontrollable client had to be effectively constrained and Buzz was the master at finding effective alternatives to decapitation.

Mr. Charrette

The HPC charrettes introduced me to a wide range of exciting projects and people during the '80s and '90s. What struck me most was the quality and talent of the team. I learned how to contribute. My role varied and involved a mix of land planning, master planning, concept design and writing. It always involved a stimulating collaborative engagement with talented HPC charrette members and introduced my firm to a range of assignments some of which are listed below:

Attractions
> Napa Valley Heritage Attraction Concept Plan, Napa, CA
> Longaberger Company Campus Concept Plan, Newark, OH
> Old Tucson Study, Tucson, AZ
> Sands Hotel Study, Las Vegas, NV
> Valencia Company Study, Six Flags Planning Area, Valencia, CA
> Milwaukee Summerfest Study, Milwaukee, WI
> Visitor Center & Commercial Complex Study, Mount St. Helens National Park, WA
> Camarillo Multi-Purpose Stadium Concept Plan, Camarillo, CA
> Great Park of Orange County, Millennium III Concept Plan, Orange County, CA
> Springfield Entertainment District Concept Plan, Springfield, MO
> Rouse Company Study, Atlantic City, NJ
> Sportopia Entertainment Center Concept Plan, Branson, MO
> Glenn's Diner & 57 Heaven Museum Concept Plan, Coachella Valley, CA
> Fess Parker Wine Center Concept Plan, Lompoc, CA

St. Martin Resort Master Planning Charrette, St. Martin Parish, LA, David A. Price Architects

Soniya Hills Resort Master Planning Charrette, Nara Prefecture, Japan, David A. Price Architects

Six Flags Movieland Master Planning Charrette, Buena Park, CA, David A. Price Architects

Resorts & Hotels

> St. Martin Resort Master Plan, St. Martin Parish, LA
> Branson Meadows Resort Master Plan, Branson, MO
> Soniya Hills Resort Master Plan, Nara Prefecture, Japan
> Monaghan Company, Long Point Resort Master Plan, Palos Verdes, CA
> Jakarta Mountain Resort Master Plan, Bojong Koneng, Indonesia
> Oita Sunrise City Resort Master Plan, Oita Prefecture, BEPP, Japan
> Waterfront Hotel Feasibility Study, Hakata Bay, Fukuoka Prefecture, Japan

The HPC charrettes introduced all of us to a kind of total abandonment focused at finding solutions to an exciting challenge. Buzz pulled together the necessary upfront talent and then went about empowering each of us with a belief that we could land the plane. It was infectious. It prepared us for life.

It's all About the Numbers and More

Dad was indeed the numbers guy that helped shape our industry, but he was certainly much more. Dad knew not only how to work the numbers, he had a special way to engage and draw from the participants and stakeholders. He did so with wit, humor, intelligence and an uncanny ability to cut through to the core question(s) at the perfect time.

Dad's penetrating questions sometimes drove me nuts as a teenager but later in life knowing the core question, the underling WHY, generally proved to be a stunningly effective tool for articulating "Yes-If" solutions for challenging problems. The HPC charrette allowed Dad to tool his craft further and along the way he created a very special legion of devoted and talented friends. That was true for all of us.

Market Place Transformations

From rural food stands to begotten waterfronts, America has witnessed the emergence and transformation of marketplace properties into attractive mixed-use urban centers drawing residents and tourists seeking family and adult recreation, relaxation and entertainment experiences. Buzz consulted on numerous marketplace oriented properties during the back half of the 20th Century involving major public and private sector development initiatives. Two locations come to mind where Buzz was involved as a consultant and where I also found myself working in close proximity.

"Festival" Marketplace – Boston

As a graduate student at Harvard in the '70s, I witnessed the rebirth of Boston's waterfront led by the opening of Faneuil Hall Marketplace spearheaded by the Rouse Company. James W. Rouse, a wildly successful real estate developer whose notable achievements include the first enclosed shopping mall east of the Mississippi and an entire city called Columbia in Maryland. He then went on to save historic downtowns by creating festival marketplaces such as Faneuil Hall in Boston. How lucky I was to have had an early post graduate job at the end of Long Wharf next to the Boston Aquarium in the heart of the city and Faneuil Hall.

James Rouse had inspired me and many others with his remark that, "The greatest piece of urban design in the United States was Disneyland." That comment resonated strongly since Disneyland was close to home in so many ways. Buzz had also gained the trust and confidence of James Rouse. ERA, the company that Dad had founded, was conducting "Festival" Marketplace Feasibility Studies for the Rouse Company. I had a chance to later meet and work with the Rouse Company who had retained HPC to conduct a charrette to address entertainment potential for the Atlantic City Gateway Corridor, exploring strategies for "repositioning" Atlantic City as a multi-function leisure and entertainment center.

Marketplace transformations occurred elsewhere, encouraged by the writings of the legendary urban planner Jane Jacobs and other visionary thought leaders and developers like the Rouse Company. Buzz and his ERA colleagues were often in the forefront preparing key economic studies that addressed market feasibility, program development, financial feasibility, revenue strategies and economic and fiscal impact analysis. These marketplace transformations didn't always unfold in city centers, along river fronts and in harbor areas.

Knott's Berry Farm – California Marketplace

Sometimes marketplace locations have humble beginnings like a farmer's food stand offering fresh produce and baked pies to families driving by. That's the story behinds Knott's Berry Farm in Buena Park, California, now a 160-acre amusement park owned by Cedar Fair. In 2017, it was the 10th most-visited theme park in North America. Knott's Berry Farm is also the most-visited theme park in the Cedar Fair chain. The park features 35 rides including roller coasters, family rides, children's rides, water rides, and historical rides, and it employs about 10,000 seasonal and full-time employees.

The theme park sits on the site of a former berry farm established by Walter and Cordelia Knott and their family. Beginning around 1920, the Knott family sold berries, berry preserves, and pies from a roadside stand along State Route 39. In 1934, the Knott's began selling fried chicken dinners in a tea room on the property, and the Knott's built several shops and other attractions to entertain visitors as they waited for a table.

In 1940, Walter Knott began constructing a replica ghost town on the property. He added several other attractions over the years, and began charging admission to the attractions in 1968. In the 1990s, following the deaths of Walter and Cordelia Knott, their children sold the theme park to Cedar Fair which has continued to expand, adding Knott's Soak City in 1999, adding rides and family attractions like Ghost Town Alive!, Camp Snoopy and Boardwalk to the original park, and California Marketplace – home to Mrs. Knott's Family Chicken Dinner Restaurant located outside the park along Beach Boulevard.

Later in my career I had the opportunity to work with Buzz and colleagues on several projects very close to Knott's including the Economic & Concept Feasibility Study for the Buena Park Entertainment Corridor and the Six Flag's Movieland Master Plan, a 15-acre entertainment center proposed for the Buena Park Wax Museum property. Other projects followed including Wild Bill's Dinner Theater Extravaganza for Rank Leisure USA and concept feasibility studies for Ripley Entertainment on several properties located north of Knott's Berry Farm, Soak City and California Marketplace. During much of that time, Harrison Price Company conducted a number of Knott's initiated assignments involving Knott's Berry Farm and other locations. While Boston's Faneuil Hall Marketplace and Knott's California Marketplace are different in their history, setting and operation, they both rely on key planning factors critical to success.

Success Factors
> Market Position
> Developer's Vision
> Designing a "Sense of Place"
> Market Innovation
> Operating Management
> Political Relationships
> Public-Private Partnership
> Risk Assessment & Management

The owners and operators of Faneuil Hall Marketplace and Knott's both turned to Buzz and his colleagues to provide critical market research and economic feasibility consulting services to help guide development. It always involved a highly collaborative team of architects, designers, economic advisors, fabricators, builders and consultants working closely with the owner, operator and public agencies to achieve successful outcomes. At both locations, the marketplace continues to evolve and grow in the midst of a dramatically shifting retail landscape while visitors and guests continue to expect memorable and compelling retail experiences.

Roller Coaster Math – The Arithmetic of the Attraction Business

"Roller Coaster Math" was the early working title for Dad's book "Walt's Revolution! By the Numbers." The title change proved to be a smart decision since words attract different audiences and "Walt's Revolution! By the Numbers" connected directly to attractions inspired readers.

"Roller Coaster Math" has other meanings and is not to be confused with the math and science of roller coasters which depend on physics to stay connected to the track and on math for calculating speed and momentum. Certainly an important calculus if you're riding a roller coaster, defying inversions, mid-air suspensions and twisting dive tracks!

Cover photo © Cjad Slate/Getty Images & © Disney Enterprises Inc. "Walt's Revolution! By the Numbers by Harrison "Buzz" Price, Published by Ripley Entertainment

The late Terry Van Gorder, former President of Knott's Berry Farm, coined the term "Roller Coaster Math" during an overseas working session with some of his staff exploring potentials for a joint venture attraction project. Buzz had completed a fast paced presentation on what kind of new investment it would take to make the project profitable. Terry referred to Dad's presentation as "Roller Coaster Math" eventually finding its way as the title in his book for Chapter 14 – "Roller Coaster Math – The Arithmetic of the Attraction Business."

"Roller Coaster Math" is foundational to the metrics of economic feasibility analysis in the attractions industry and involved an all-new analytical vocabulary that is today the mathematical language of attraction development. Dad in short invented it. It's been refined and elaborated upon by others but it started with his work for Walt and Roy Disney and those who followed. It measures and anticipates performance in a range of subjects that include:

> Site analysis
> Concept development and positioning
> Market, size, resident, tourist and pass-through
> Market penetration
> Benchmark performance and adjustments
> Attendance projection
> Seasonality
> Design day attendance
> Peak on-site crowd at design day
> Length of visitor stay
> Ride, site and facility capacities
> Projected warranted investment, hard and soft
> Per capita expenditures
> Probable economic performance

Camp Snoopy Children's Ride & Play Attraction, ©Cedar Fair, Cedar Point, Sandusky, Ohio (1999). Architect - David A. Price Architects, Inc.

As Dad points out in his book, the key to the above were two factors that got better over time. First, numbers practitioners built up extensive data banks and libraries concerning the performance of projects. Second, sharpened intuition that comes from doing this type of work in the entertainment field for a long period. As important as the data was, you had to have good sense! What's obscured is a simple truth that Dad would often say – most of the analysis uses skills in math and algebra you mastered in the lower grades and high school.

For the attractions practitioner, the best way to get a foundational understanding of the arithmetic of the attraction industry is to turn to Chapter 14 entitled "Roller Coaster Math." Dad wrote like he talked – straight forward, colorful sidebar stories with highly informative insights. What's amazing is that prior to Walt and Roy, it was pretty much a gut check. Buzz de-mystified it. Roller Coaster Math provided common sense logic and enabled Dad to mathematically quantify for investors, creators, and operators, the meaningful business investment opportunity.

While the math and formulas continue to be tweaked, the principles and philosophies were all pioneered by Buzz Price. As Buzz made clear in his book, there's nothing secret about these formulas even though there seems to be a mystery around them.

> **Expected annual attendance:** _____
> **Peak Month:** 21.25% of expected annual attendance = _____
> **Peak Week:** Divide Peak Month by 4.3 (the average number of weeks per month) = _____
> **Peak Day:** 25% of peak week = _____
> **Design Day:** 18.5% of your peak week = _____
> **Peak On-Site:** Design Day _____ x .75 = _____

Design day numbers shown should not be seen as actual figures because they vary tremendously based on a variety of factors including attraction type, market, location, seasonality, weather, school schedules, length of stay, etc. For example, a waterpark might have a 30% or even 35% peak month, whereas a theme park in a year-round market like Orlando might have an 18% peak month. Likewise, a theme park might have peak on site of 80%, whereas a museum could have 25%. Peak Day and Design Day also vary depending on the extent to which the market is resident or tourist oriented (resident markets get more weekend attendance thus bumping up peak day). In addition, an analysis today might use more complicated algorithms based on econometrics and big data. Having said that, industry analysis still relies on both art (professional judgement) and science.

Buzz's roller coaster math was also directed at measuring the impact of the attraction business. At a Governor's Conference on Tourism in 1998, Buzz provided a short form method to compute the impact of the attraction business:

$$I = (GRi + Eo) M$$

Where annual impact (I) is the sum of gross revenues inside the gate (GRi) plus tourist visitor expenditures outside the gate (Eo) both multiplied by an appropriate multiplier (M) based on leakage estimates (percentage spent outside the impact area).

Multipliers for leakage are mathematically computed as follows:

Leakage (%)	Multiplier
30	3.33
35	2.86
40	2.50
50	1.99

Thus, if for $200 million we can create an attraction drawing 3 million people, spending $30 each, attracting 40 percent tourists spending $500 per day, extending stay time 1/2 day, and do it with 40 percent leakage, the annual impact is:

$$I = [(3,000,000) (30) + (3,000,000) (0.4) (50/2)] \, 2.50$$
$$I = [120,000,000] \, [2.50] = \$300 \text{ million}$$

The example Buzz presented may be somewhat simplistic, but it pointed to how an example returns $300 million annually to its impact area on a project costing $200 million. Of course, the economic impact multipliers are entirely dependent on the local economy in which the attraction is located. For example, New York would have an entirely different multiplier than Boise. The stronger the regional economy, the less economic activity leaks out of the area, and the higher the multiplier.

That's Roller Coaster Math!

A Numbers Guide to Laughter

Dad used numbers as a means for finding humor in life. He was hard wired that way. My hardest laughs were with dad sometimes at 30,000 feet returning home from a business trip. We could laugh till our eyes cried, the stomach muscles ached, and the flight attendant would cast a concerning glance. It could also happen on a lift chair heading back up the mountain. Ask my brother Bret. There was no subject that couldn't be unmasked. Ask anyone that worked with Buzz and you'll find similar stories about sharing a comedic moment or group laugh with him.

In my architectural career I had been retained by several pastors around the country to master plan their community churches. I was an "unchurched" architect that somehow found resonance with pastors open to my unorthodox approach. After all, if you are going to grow a church, shouldn't you be trying to connect with the unchurched? If you're not growing, you're just stealing from someone else.

I found my church clients and their members to be a fun group, especially if they didn't introduce identity politics and taking it one more step was open minded about spirits especially a good cabernet. Maybe I had found a niche. Dynamic pastors also used humor to tell their stories. It's an effective tool for connecting. Just preaching had its limits.

The humor was not lost on family and friends. Dad got it. It was a promising market with lots of story potential. It prompted a conversation I once had with a pastor friend about laughter and fellowship. He remarked that laughter was sometimes another form of prayer. I thought if this were the case, I was praying a lot more than I realized and so were my friends in the entertainment industry.

Dad used laughter to shed light on the numbers. His humor and wit are also what we remember.

Community of Joy, Kid Kountry Daycare Center, Glendale, AZ – Gold Nugget Design Award, David A. Price Architects

Life Christian Church, Worship & Welcome Center, West Orange, NJ, David A. Price Architects

Pinon Hills Community Church, Worship & Welcome Center, Farmington, NM – LEED Silver, David A. Price Architects

Buzz & Annie at Wine Tasting Party, Los Angeles, '80s

Buzz and Annie, early '40s

Buzz & Annie vacationing
in Scotland, '90s

Annie & Buzz at David and Alicia's home in
Orange County, CA, 2006

High Altitude Love Letters

If you knew my father, you knew my mother. By any measure theirs was an authentic romance. It can easily be said that Annie was the glue to it all. Dad knew this to be true with absolute clarity. In his later years airborne at 30,000 feet, suspended between destinations with time to kill, dad took note in his three-ring binder about the time he met Annie in April 1941.

"She was 18 and I was 20. She was (and is) a compassionate liberal. Intelligent (she clobbers me at gin and crossword puzzles); sensitive to the core; caring in excess; committing without reservation; gorgeous through the years. Where was the Pomona competition? Better looking, more grown up (than me). They were happily near sighted. She was worthy of artists, leaders, princes, presidents, teachers and statesmen – the best of men. And she latched on to me with an enthusiasm that terrified her parents and she gave me a combination of artificial respiration and inspiration that breathed fire into my immature psycho-structure and I grew up. Without her I would have been at the mercy of chance with limited odds."

My father's pronouncements of his love for mom were often expressed at home but it flourished at high altitude. On a flight from Amsterdam and Frankfurt, Oct. 23, 1975, he wrote again:

"How was it cut out that I should find Mecca in the mating game? A frightened, over compensating, self-centered, preciously narcissistic, over focused marginal man – a parochial yokel like me; saved by a sexual and spiritual bar mitzvah with a soulful woman – a reservoir – an oasis – redemption. It was a miracle."

What a blessing it is to have been raised in a home where the love that existed between these two love birds was what lifted us from our nest. It had enough force and presence to lift all of us: family, friends and colleagues.

It's an example of how sometimes 1 + 1 = 3. Buzz the "Numbers Guy" knew it.

IAAPA Hall of Fame Inductee

The International Association of Amusement Parks and Attractions (IAAPA) inducted Buzz into its prestigious Hall of Fame in November 1995. His close friend and colleague Marty Sklar, himself a Hall of Fame inductee, shared an industry wide sentiment about Buzz's inclusion: "We're all so fortunate that Walt Disney had a 'Numbers Man' who loved music, art, and poetry." It was a Numbers Guy with a love for the arts that as Bob Roger's put it, "Increased the core competency of our entire industry for generations to come."

Annie made sure she was by his side the day Buzz received his IAAPA Hall of Fame award.

The IAAPA honor was part of other industry recognitions that Dad would enjoy during the later part of his life. As delighted as he was by the recognition, he always remained "Dad" at the home front and "Buzz" for those that knew and worked with him. Mom was pretty much the same person too, whether she was talking with a young mother with small children on a dirt floor or in elegant surrounding with well healed folks.

Dad passed away on August 15, 2010, just a month after visiting and speaking at The Walt Disney Family Museum. Several months later still feeling the fresh emotions from the passing of my father, I was again at IAAPA EXPO in Orlando, where I followed a goodwill trail lined by friends and colleagues of my father and Annie – all expressing kind words and sharing stories.

It was a very memorable time for me that underscored what I already knew. Dad loved being part of a community of people whose DNA was focused at putting smiles on the faces of people. Buzz the Numbers Guy knew how to help an attraction industry and the people that comprised it to achieve greater success. He energized them by helping to elevate their game and in turn they energized him.

One could easily say that Buzz was the right person in the right place at the right time. He also understood that luck is a wild card in life and that his story could have easily been different. He mentioned to me once that it was only by chance that he didn't end up on the front lines of the Battle of the Bulge, the last major German offensive campaign on the Wester Front during World War II where thousands were killed and wounded.

What changed his circumstance on that occasion was the luck-of-the-draw – he was quick with numbers so the military pulled him from the ranks that would ultimately head to Germany so that he might apply his analytic skills elsewhere in the military.

IAAPA was home to many close friends of Buzz and Annie. While some have passed away, many others remain along with their memorable stories stemming from shared travel experiences, work assignments and many hours of laughter. Buzz was truly honored to be inducted into IAAPA's Hall of Fame, joining many of his friends, including Walt Disney, Bob Rogers, Walter Knott, George Millay, and Marty Sklar.

Disney Legend

Perhaps more than any other recognition or award that Dad received, the Disney Legends Award on Oct. 16, 2003, was a hallmark achievement deeply felt and appreciated by him. Buzz helped Walt Disney hand-pick the optimum locations for Disneyland in 1953 and Walt Disney World in 1963 among other projects. He became one of Walt's most trusted advisors. Michael Eisner credited Dad with being "as much responsible for the success of The Walt Disney Company as anybody except Walt Disney himself."

The Disney Legends Award is the highest honor The Walt Disney Company can bestow on an individual. It is reserved for those few who have truly made an indelible mark on the history of the company.

Dad's professional and personal life had been forever changed and enriched by his relationship to Walt and Roy Disney and we all had been benefactors of it. Joining Mom and Dad at Disney Legends Plaza at The Walt Disney Studios for the ceremony was indeed a very happy and joyful occasion.

Harrison "Buzz" Price and Roy Disney, California Institute of the Arts, Valencia, CA

Left to right, Walt Disney, CV Wood & Harrison "Buzz" Price
looking at early plans for Disneyland

David Smith, Walt Disney Co. Archivist (retired) and Buzz

My friend and colleague Andrea Favilli who had worked as a concept designer for Walt Disney Imagineering, had been charged with the task of designing the original Legends Award given in 1989. Inspired by the work of Herb Ryman, who had designed Sleeping Beauty Castle in Disneyland during the early 1950s, Andrea focused on designing an award fit for a Disney Legend. He recalls, "As I thought about it, three key elements came to mind: an amazing imagination; two, an inherent skill or talent; and three, an adept way of combining imagination with skill to create magic."

Dad, dean of entertainment attractions consulting and trusted advisor to Walt, possessed all three qualities Andrea described, imagination, talent and magic (when 1 + 1 = 3!). Metrics and numbers were Dad's paint brushes and he was now and always will be a Disney Legend.

CalArts

Later in his extraordinary life, Walt Disney conceived of a new school for nurturing future generations of creative talent: a multidisciplinary "community of the arts" built around the real-life experience of working artists instead of the conventions of the academy. His vision began to take shape in 1961 with the incorporation of California Institute of the Arts, known by its nickname CalArts. Ten years later, CalArts moved into its new campus in Valencia, California.

The school became the first degree-granting institution of higher learning in the United States created specifically for students of both the visual and performing arts. It offers Bachelor of Fine Arts, Master of Fine Arts, Master of Arts, and Doctor of Musical Arts degrees among six disciplines: Art; Critical Studies; Dance; Film/Video; Music; and Theater.

The launching of CalArts took place during the tumultuous era of the '60s, a time when my siblings and I were also in our teens. Whether around the dinner table or amongst family friends involved in the school, CalArts was often a part of the conversation. While I didn't know it at the time, CalArts had already acquired Chouinard where I had taken pre-college studies in Painting and Drawing in 1964 and 1965. A decade later, my brother Bret would attend CalArts receiving his Master of Arts in 1975. In the years that followed, Bret would emerge in his own right as a nationally renowned artist and sculptor, his work now part of major private collections and museums throughout the country.

Walt Disney died before seeing CalArts become a reality, but he left his vision in the hands of someone he was confident would make it happen – Buzz Price. Disney Legend Marty Sklar spoke at a Buzz Price Celebration at CalArts on October 12, 2010, just a few months after Dad's passing.

"I was thinking about how best to characterize the talents, dedication and achievements of this self-described "Numbers

Donn Tatum, Card Walker, Harrison "Buzz" Price, John Kelsey and Thornton Ladd with Walt Disney (photograph courtesy California Institute of the Arts), © Disney

Man" – and it occurred to me that it's a shame Buzz did not make a career in the military.

Think if it, Buzz would have made a great General. His credentials: Chief Executive of three companies, Chairman of the Board of CalArts, President of the Los Angeles Master Chorale, Co-Founder of Ryman Arts.

He would have made a great First Sergeant. His credentials: Organizing and marching his staff – his Army – through the analysis of more than 3,000 economic feasibility studies in the leisure / recreation, theme park and attraction industries for just about every major player: Disney, Knott's, Universal, Sea World, Six Flags, museums, zoos and eight World's Fairs. They called what Buzz did "Roller coaster Math."

And Buzz would have been a great Private First Class – a foot soldier, as he was when Walt Disney and Roy O. Disney asked him in 1953, "To determine the economic feasibility of the best location for a new project, Disneyland."

But despite his amazing worldly accomplishments, no place on earth meant more to Buzz Price than CalArts – its students and its faculty and administrators. And no one followed orders, as a good military person must, more completely and effectively than Buzz did.

Walt Disney's daughter, Diane Disney Miller, told me this story about a conversation that happened the day before Walt entered the hospital in 1966, Diane said," Dad placed a stack of notebooks in Buzz's hands, and said: 'Here, take care of my school for me!' Dad

California Institute of the Arts, Valencia, California (Photograph courtesy California Institute of the Arts)

Artist, Bret Price, "High Hopes", 2004, painted steel, 20 ft. high

knew, Diane said, "The right hands to place his dream in, that Buzz would see it through, and he did!"

Buzz, military or not, we salute you! We would not be here today without you! Whether we are film, theatre or theme park fans, we all thank our lucky stars that Walt Disney had a "Numbers Man" who loved music, art and poetry."

In later years, I often told Dad that with all his accomplishments, working to make CalArts a reality might prove to be his "Living" legacy.

Walt expressed similar words when he said "CalArts is the principal thing I hope to leave when I move on to greener pastures. If I can help provide a place to develop the talent of the future, I think I will have accomplished something."

The Buzz Price Thea Award – Recognizing a Lifetime of Distinguished Achievements

How is it that the Themed Entertainment Association (TEA) representing creators of compelling places and experiences worldwide would honor a "Numbers Guy" upon his passing by naming its Lifetime Achievement Award in his name – Buzz Price Thea Award for a Lifetime of Distinguished Achievements?

Harrison "Buzz" Price, was the first recipient and single honoree of TEA's Thea Awards in 1994. A year later, the Thea Awards would again celebrate a single honoree, Walt Disney Imagineering's Marty Sklar. By 1996, TEA introduced the Awards for Outstanding Achievement (AOA), turning the Thea Awards into a multi-award event.

From the start and to this day, the objective of the Thea Awards is simple: To find excellence and celebrate it. The Thea Awards honors the entire achievement and everyone who worked on the achievement, rather than individuals. While the Buzz Price Thea Award for a Lifetime of Distinguished Achievement recognizes the excellence of a person's lifetime of work, honorees know very well how their achievements spring from special opportunities supported by the talent and hard work from others. What's truly recognized is the leadership, creative imagination and inspirational impact that each Buzz Price Thea Award recipient brings to the themed entertainment industry. Where would we be without them? Buzz was there to usher in a new era and others followed.

Buzz and the company that he founded Economics Research Associates (now AECOM), spawned legions of economists who today help guide a world-wide entertainment attractions industry. But no one should be misled. For Buzz, it was never just about the numbers. It was a means to an end.

Buzz used numbers as a creative spark enabling and empowering a broad community of investors, creators and operators, and creating a watershed for the world's theme park and themed entertainment industries in the 20th Century. Buzz's "roller coaster math" provided the metrics for measuring the return on investment allowing an entertainment industry to come together to focus its energy and talent around a higher purpose – putting smiles on the faces of children, families and people across the globe.

Harrison "Buzz" Price Window Dedication – April 9, 2013

Dad passed away in 2010 and Mom followed two years later. Just before Mom's passing, Marty Sklar, a close friend of the family and a Disney Legend himself, called to say that Dad would be honored with his own "Window" at Disneyland.

Left to right, Tom Skaggs, David Price & Michael Colglazier at Harrison "Buzz" Price Window Dedication, Disneyland, Anaheim, CA, April 9, 2013, © Disney

Price Family siblings, left to right David Price, Dana Price, Holly Ristuccia & Bret Price at Harrison "Buzz" Price Window Dedication, Disneyland, Anaheim, CA, April 9, 2013, Mickey Mouse © Disney

A "Disney Window" is a lifetime achievement award for those who contributed in some pioneering way to the Disney parks. Those honored are determined by corporate leadership and are extended only to retired individuals. Their window treatment typically appears as a fictitious business and often refers to their role or some hobby of theirs.

The inscription on Dad's window reads. "Harrison "Buzz" Price, Founder & Finder." It was a joyous blue-sky morning dedication just before the park opened. Dad and Mom's presence was deeply felt. My brother and sisters along with our children, family friends and the press were all in attendance for the dedication that took place in front of the park's City Hall where Dad's "Window" was installed. Afterward family and grandchildren enjoyed Disney FASTPASS, skipping ride lines for both parks and ending their day when the parks closed.

Dad always said how lucky he was. Life is fickle. It helps to be prepared. Buzz was the right man at the right time. Buzz's special brand of humor, wit, passion and intelligence resonated with two brothers that together launched a revolution in family entertainment and destination attractions. Buzz's "Yes If" approach to creative thinking allowed Walt and Roy to move forward with their ideas in a manner that changed our world. This "Yes If" approach also proved to be essential for giving direction and balance to a dynamic and creative attractions industry inspired by the vision and success of Walt Disney.

Where did Buzz's "Yes If" approach spring from? He most certainly understood its practical dimensions as a consultant, but he also appreciated its application when you're surrounded by creative thinkers and visionaries. While Buzz could drill down into numbers with a focus that boarded on obsession, he also knew how to translate numbers and economic data into meaningful and easily understood terms.

By any measure, he was the perfect fit for Walt and Walt's brother

Harrison "Buzz" Price Window
at City Hall, Disneyland, CA

Roy and continued to be so over the years for wide ranging Disney initiatives that changed the global landscape in the world of destination resorts and parks.

This "Yes If" approach combined with his intelligence, common sense and experience enabled him to mathematically quantify for investors, creators and operators the meaningful business investment opportunity used to guide the development of Disneyland, Walt Disney World, other theme parks and wide ranging cultural, education and sports related projects.

It all began in Anaheim, the city that Buzz recommended as the best location for Disneyland. With Walt's encouragement Buzz also met with Gene Autry with the purpose of bringing the Angels Major League Baseball franchise to Anaheim. The opening of Disneyland represented a new era for Orange County and the dawn of an exciting and robust creative economy driven by the arts, design and entertainment.

Today that creative economy ranks fourth out of 66 industry clusters in greater Los Angeles, supporting one in eight jobs in the region and a regional creative economy output of $190 billion in 2017. Buzz hit the bull's eye when he selected Anaheim as the best site for Disneyland and he's honored with a "Window" at City Hall for doing so.

Lessons I Learned from Buzz

As my own life unfolded professionally and personally, Dad was my go-to guy for advice. It was the same for others. Sometimes it was a half hour visit in his office, a five-minute chat on the phone, hanging by the pool with wives and grandchildren, or flying with Buzz to and fro at 30,000 feet on assignment. Whether for me and my siblings, an industry colleague or a young professional in between jobs, the takeaway was often the same:

1) **Find your passion**
2) **Stay focused**
3) **Work hard**
4) **Don't stop**
5) **Have fun!**

And remember, whether you're raising kids, changing a tire or building a bridge:

"The language of 'Yes-If' is more conducive to solving problems; 'No-Because' is a deal breaker." – Buzz Price

CHAPTER 13

What Would Buzz Do?

BY David A. Price AIA

Dad loved to write and give speeches to industry groups. He would craft a speech tailored to the audience, send me a copy, often with hand notes, and over time they grew into a personal collection that I still enjoy returning to. I still marvel at his wit, humor and depth of knowledge. With preparation and knowledge in hand, he could laser into the topic in a manner that was his own and entertain the audience

The speeches often contained "Lists" like "Rules for Strategic Planning & Intelligent Action," "Guidelines for Contemporary Ethical Business Practices" and "Criteria for Taking an Entrepreneur's Plunge." The lists would find their way into his speeches at roundtable lunches and business groups. The common thread – personal stories that introduced the subject matter, industry information that included demographic data and market trends, sample projects and technologies demonstrating fresh ideas and approaches, and at some point, a humor laden "List" of what to do (or not). You always learned something and had a good laugh.

What Would Buzz Do?

With so many careers and lives impacted by Buzz's contribution to the attractions industry, it's only fitting to ask the question – "What Would Buzz Do?" So, here's my answer:

> **Know yourself**
> **Become a complete person**
> **Find balance in your life**
> **Stay real, humanistic and holistic**
> **Find humor in the journey**
> **Above all, SERVE**

Sounds old fashioned, but those are the qualities that Buzz is remembered for by friends and colleagues that knew him well. Mom and Dad modeled those qualities at home and in their civic life where public and community service was a rewarding and fulfilling expression of who they were. It drew family and friends into a world where art, music, theater, comedy, education and sports had value and purpose.

Prior to Walt Disney's passing, he entrusted Dad to help guide the founding and launch of California Institute of the Arts (CalArts) in Valencia, California. When Herbert Ryman passed away, a close friend and legendary Imagineer at Walt Disney Studios, Dad and Mom along with Marty & Leigh Sklar, Sharon D. Lund and Lucille Ryman Carroll founded Ryman Arts, a nationally recognized arts education program for talented high school students in Los Angeles, California. Mom and Dad were also lifelong lovers of music which led to board roles and support for the Los Angeles Master Chorale. Their commitment to service and community engagement also extended to the planning and support of the Los Angeles Olympics in 1984. All these efforts brought music, art and sports into our home and impacted the lives of so many others.

To answer "What Would Buzz Do?" you simply have to appreciate how Buzz lived his life. These outside interests and passions were what completed Buzz as a person, connecting him to a community of friends and colleagues in all aspects of his life.

Flags & Rags

Of course, questions often lead to multiple answers. As a teenager, "What Would Buzz Do?" wasn't what I usually asked. It reminds me of a story when Dad and I had a run in.

It was 1968, a turbulent year in a violent era. Home was only an hour away by car from Pomona College where I was majoring in art and completing core liberal arts classes. I would return home once in a while to graze much like my own children have done. We lived in a beautiful home in the middle of Hancock Park a few houses from Mayor Bradley and the Chandlers, owner of the Los Angeles Times. Our neighborhood was akin to an arboretum with towering trees and canopies stretching across quiet neighborhood streets. Music from our times would echo through our home. Art work from Disney artists and others adorned our walls.

I had gone into our expansive garage in a creative mood looking around for materials. I grabbed some old curtains, American flags, cans of paint and a plywood panel that I used for backing and just started to make something. We had fiberglass and resin used to patch surfboards which I used as a binder. After I was finished and the fiberglass had set, I cut the irregular edges of the piece that was roughly three by four feet overall. It looked like the residue of battle, a war gone wrong at least to my innocent eyes so far removed from the front line. The American flags were torn and shredded and the spattered red paint evoked the wounds of war.

Dad was furious when he saw what I had done and my furry shot back just as strongly. Mom called for a Red Flag Truce – a family rule – that quieted angry voices when things said had gone too far.

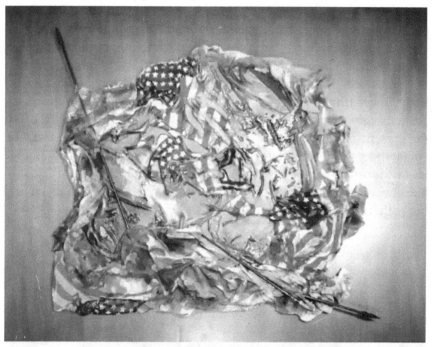

Flags & Rags, Fiberglass Montage, 30"x40" by David Price, 1968

What I've never forgotten is how Dad handled it. By evening, the art work hang on a commanding wall at home in the family room where it stayed until the house was sold many years later. Dad had turned his anger, really our anger, and flipped it. He could sometimes be quick to anger but could let go. He could be hyper focused but knew how to listen. He understood that acknowledgment was healing and important. Lessons from home!

The Question Behind the Question

I'm reminded of other stories from home that answer the question, "What would Buzz do?" Each has a different answer. If there's a lesson in any of them, it's understanding the question behind the question – the why. Dad had a way of challenging his kids with a question rather than a command. It might be laced with humor. At times it might have a bit of a bark to it. But the question usually lingered and forced you to keep thinking about it.

Later in life, as a practicing architect and working in a collaborative environment, knowing the core question was key to your purpose and outcome. Dad had an amazing ability to zero in on the key question(s) in a planning charrette and that was empowering to the entire team. He also knew how to select talented, creative thinkers that could help flush out the key questions that in turn lead to creative solutions to complex challenges. "What Would Buzz do?" is the question that leads to another question. The Why behind the purpose.

Buzz was a very complete person. Not in all ways, but in ways that allowed him to gain the trust from others, to weigh the nature of a particular set of challenges, to find ways to understand it metrically in the present and in the future, and to translate it in a manner that others could understand, appreciate and use to generate successful outcomes. It led to transformational change. His life lesson to each of us is to become as complete a person as you can be and embrace what you are not with humor, love and humility.

Harrison "Buzz" Price, HPC Home/Office, San Pedro, CA, mid-'90s

Acknowledgements

Friends and colleagues who worked with Buzz on HPC charrettes as well as other client projects share a certain kind of fellowship often born from long flights, long nights, complex clients, challenging time constraints, etc. Buzz extended his trust and confidence to each of us and in turn we responded with our best.

HPC's independent outside panel of experts would interact with in-house HPC talent on the specifics of project development. While the panels varied, a core group of talent grew. The assembled "Buzz" Stories come from those who built bonds working together in response to exciting and challenging assignments emerging from HPC and other firms.

I wish to acknowledge my colleagues and their associated companies who continue to provide key economic feasibility consulting services and whose lives and professional histories have been inspired and impacted by my father: starting with the company he founded, Economics Research Associates (now AECOM); John Robinett, Senior VP – Economics at AECOM; the principals that formed the core practice of Harrison Price Company (HPC); and others who launched economic consulting companies like Ray Braun at ECA, Mark Dvorchak at ProForma Advisors LLC; and Jill Bensley at JB Research. I also want to thank my friend and colleague Tim O'Brien of Casa Flamingo Literary Arts for his editing help and direction.

Finally, I wish to acknowledge my father – Harrison "Buzz" Price – the recognized dean of themed entertainment consulting and our leader. For those who worked with Buzz and knew him, he was always more than a "Numbers Guy." He was a highly intelligent creative man that saw numbers as a means to an end where life lessons were learned.

Bob Rogers

Founder & Chief Creative Officer
BRC Imagination Arts

"I first met Buzz Price in 1971 while he was still running the original ERA. I was a student at CalArts. Not right away, but eventually he became a mentor to me. He and I worked together on quite a number of projects, boards and committees. He was always the master and I was always the student." – Bob Rogers

Storyteller, inventor, writer, and more, Bob Rogers is the founder and chairman of BRC Imagination Arts, which has become known for reinventing brand homes, visitor centers, and museums for the 21st Century. BRC's past clients include NASA, Disney, General Motors, Ford, Coca-Cola, Heineken, Jameson, Amore Pacific, Heineken, China Mobile and more.

Since its inception in 1981, BRC's projects have been honored with over 350 international awards for creative excellence, including two Academy Award Nominations and 21 Thea Awards for Outstanding Achievement in themed entertainment. NASA invited Bob to help develop its master plan for the exploration of Mars. He was later awarded the NASA Public Service Medal.

Bob is a member of the Academy of Motion Picture Arts and Sciences (the Oscars®) and served on the Academy's Board of Directors from 2014 to 2017.

Like Buzz, Bob is a recipient of both the Thea Award for Lifetime Achievement and an inductee into the IAAPA Hall of Fame. Buzz and Bob served together on the Board of the Ryman Arts Foundation, providing scholarships for young artists of exceptional talent.

Michael V. Lee

MLD Productions (retired)
Producer/Director, Planner, Designer & Architect

For more than 40 years in the Experience Industry, Michael Lee has built a reputation for excellence in producing high-visibility, world-class projects. His work includes museums, theme parks, cultural entertainment centers, water parks, resorts, theaters, retail-dining-entertainment (RD&E) centers and other types of experience-based leisure, recreation and education projects.

In the early 1970s he was a professor of Art & Design at California State University, Fullerton, where he advocated "Design Thinking," was Chair of the Faculty Senate Committee on Institutional Research and Computing Facilities, and was the co-founder of the Environmental Studies Department, one of the first successful interdisciplinary environment-oriented programs of its kind in the US. As Director of Design for Lucas Arts Attractions, a division of Industrial Light and Magic (a George Lucas Company now owned by Walt Disney Co.) he lead a team of world-class producers, planners and designers creating attractions for Universal Studios and other major entertainment companies.

In 1989 Michael launched Michael Lee Design / MLD Productions for consulting, planning, designing, constructing and managing projects for a wide variety of clients worldwide, including Warner Bros., Children's Television Workshop (now Sesame Workshop), Atlantis Resorts, Smithsonian Institution, and the Polynesian Cultural Center.

His awards include honors from the Hong Kong Downtown Merchants Association and he has been honored for "Innovation in the Use of New Materials" by General Electric Company and was the recipient of the Utah Governor's Award for Excellence.

Patrick R. Scanlon

President,
PRS Associates, Inc

Pat Scanlon has extensive experience in planning, designing and producing world-class destination projects including resorts, theme parks, visitor centers, museums, resorts and theme parks. He's also an experienced developer asset manager for investor-owned commercial real estate properties in Arizona and Colorado and is a development partner in a $100 million mixed-use retail center in Colorado Springs. He has also served as president and COO of a start-up international, long-distance telephone service provider and has intimate knowledge of 480 Holdings, Ltd., where he is both an investor, member of the Board of Managers and COO.

Prior to moving to Colorado, Pat spent 18 years with Walt Disney Imagineering where he held positions of Senior Vice President, Project Management (U.S. and Japan); Senior Vice President, Epcot Development; Vice President and General Manager, Creative Group (Concept, Design, Engineering and Manufacturing); and Vice President, Business and Marketing Development.

Pat received his bachelor's degree in economics from the University of California at Santa Barbara and his master's degree in finance from the UCLA Graduate School of Management. He has served as an international board member of the Themed Entertainment Association (TEA), Chairman of the TEA's Awards Committee, board member of The Learning Company, Chairman of the Angeles Chorale in Los Angeles and Chairman & President of the National Space Science & Technology Institute in Colorado Springs.

Jill Bensley

President,
JB Research Company

Jill Bensley is president of JB Research Company, an economic consulting firm specializing in concept development, market and financial feasibility testing for cultural, retail, entertainment, and sports real estate projects. Though trained as an economist, she has long believed that the big hits and all of the "misses" in these industries are a function of understanding and catering to the collective hearts and minds of various demographic cohorts. Because of this belief, she is an avid trend watcher and an expert on characteristics and behavior of various market segments.

She has more than 25 years of experience in the economic planning and research industry, beginning with her work with Economics Research Associates in Los Angeles. At Federated Department Stores she served as Research Analyst and was Director of Research for South Mark/University Group, a multi-million-dollar real estate firm. She was Vice President of Harrison Price Company in Los Angeles before establishing JB Research Company.

Active in her surrounding community, she is a co-founder of Kids' Arts, an arts education program for children in foster care in Ventura County. She currently serves as an appointed member of the Economic Vitality Commission in Ventura County and has taught real estate market analysis at UCLA and UCSB.

Jill's clients include the Kellogg Company, the Coca Cola Company, Legoland Theme Parks, the Academy of Motion Picture Arts and Sciences, Sega Corporation, Sony Development, American Girl Place, The Children's Place, Nintendo Corporation of America, Nickelodeon, CNN, Gaylord Entertainment, and the Portland Trail Blazers.

Sharon J. Dalrymple

Senior VP,
Harrison Price Company (retired)

Sharon (Shari) Dalrymple is a former Senior Vice President of Harrison Price Company. Before she retired in 2009, she spent more than 40 years as an economic analyst specializing in entertainment industry feasibility studies, with particular emphasis on major museums and other nonprofit enterprises. Among her clients were the Smithsonian Institution, for which she completed landmark studies for the National Museum of the American Indian, the National Air & Space Museum, the National Museum of Natural History, the Museum of Science & Industry in Chicago, the Texas State History Museum in Austin, Johnson Space Center in Houston and the Aquarium of the Americas in New Orleans.

Born in the little fishing village of Port Townsend, Washington, Shari moved with her family to the Los Angeles area at an early age. She attended schools in the San Fernando Valley and went on to acquire a degree in music composition and theory from the University of California at Los Angeles, graduating cum laude in 1965. While a student there, she was an editor of the UCLA yearbook, president of her sorority, and a member of the women's intramural golf team.

Her love of nature and personal interest in wildlife photography has taken her to such far-flung destinations as East Africa, the Australian Outback, Amazonia, the Galapagos Islands, and Micronesia. She now remains closer to her current home near Sacramento and enjoys gardening, bird-watching, reading, genealogy research, and writing about wildlife, for which she has won several awards.

Adam Krivatsy, AIA, AICP

Strategic Planner &
Real Estate Advisor

Adam Krivatsy is an architect and urban planner with more than 40 years of international consulting experience. In 1967, he was a founding Principal of Hart Krivatsy Stubee, a multidisciplinary professional firm now serving its clients as Hart Howerton, under the leadership of David Howerton, ASLA, AICP. Semi-retired, today Adam consults with principals and staff of Hart Howerton.

He spent much of his professional career advising selected clients: elected and appointed officials and public agencies responsible for improving cities, promoting economic development through tourism and in a responsible management of environmental resources; and private developers or land trusts dedicated to responsible management of their real estate assets.

Adam led professional teams in planning successful destination resorts and regions, including Walt Disney World in Florida, Callaway Gardens in Georgia, Napa Valley's Silverado Golf Resort and Conference Center, Ka'anapali Beach Resort on the Hawaiian island of Maui, and the expanded Mauna Kea Resort on the Big Island of Hawaii.

He is a long-standing member of the Urban Land Institute (ULI), the American Institute of Architects (AIA), and the American Institute of Certified Planners (AICP). Appointed to the faculties of the Schools of Architecture of the Polytechnical University of Budapest and Columbia University of New York, he taught graduate courses in Planning of New Cities, Urban Redevelopment and Advanced Urban Design.

Barry Howard

President / Creative Director
Barry Howard Limited

A pioneer in the field of Interpretive Design, Barry has achieved international prominence through the creation and design of myriad cultural attractions, museums, visitor centers, world's fair pavilions and major exhibitions for more than 50 years. Trained in fine art and scenic design, he brings to the interpretive/experience design profession a strong sense of dramatic environment and a special insight into the psychology of audience response.

Barry's sensitivity to the evolution of storyline-driven attractions combined with his insightful historical perspective provides the foundation upon which his practice has, over the course of myriad projects chronicled the American experience and explored the future horizon. In addition, his propensity for thinking "outside the box" and adapting cutting-edge communications technology to user-friendly, interactive and immersive experiences has become legendary in the design profession.

His expertise encompasses all design disciplines---form, structure, graphics, film, digital video and the written word---as well as all phases of project development. Over the course of his career, he has brought these skills to bear on a broad spectrum of significant educational attractions, from The American Freedom Train, the nation's most successful Bicentennial exhibition, to the world-renowned California State Railroad Museum in Sacramento, California and the Mississippi River Museum in Memphis Tennessee.

Today, as participatory media becomes increasingly sophisticated and the demand for cultural attractions expands throughout the world, Barry Howard Limited remains in the vanguard of the Interpretive/ Experience Design Profession.

Michael C. Mitchell

Founder & President
MCM Group

Michael C. Mitchell is an American planner, designer, lecturer and environmentalist. His work focuses primarily on the planning and design of destinations, attractions, leisure and rural development.

His company MCM Group is an international planning and design firm headquartered in Los Angeles. Founded in 1984 by Michael after the close of the Los Angeles Olympic Games, where he served as the head of planning and operations, the firm has sought to expand those planning techniques as a model to address prominent social problems. Michael has developed offices in Tokyo, Moscow, Middle East offices in Doha, Qatar, Nairobi, Kenya and currently four offices in China.

At Portland State University, he became one of the organizers of the First Earth Day in 1970, coordinating universities throughout America's northwest states. After his work on the first Earth Day, he was one of 10 university students selected from across the nation by President Richard Nixon's Administration to form a national Youth Advisory Board on environmental matters. He continued his work with what became the United States Environmental Protection Agency (EPA), writing an environmental education program for students.

In the early 1980s Michael was recruited by the Los Angeles Olympic Organizing Committee, where he served as the Group Vice-President of Planning and Control (Finance). During the Olympics he was responsible for the Games Operations Center and oversaw the closeout of the Games after their completion. He has since served as a senior planning consultant to six other Olympic Games and four world fairs.

Nick Winslow

President, Nick Winslow Consultant
International Recreation & Facilities Services

Nick Winslow was born in Los Angeles and is a proud fourth generation Angelino. He graduated from South Pasadena High School and earned a BA from Pomona College and an MBA from the Stanford Graduate School of Business. After a stint in the Air Force he began his career at Economics Research Associates in Los Angeles, where he developed a practice in the field of leisure time economics while developing the firm's offices in Washington, DC, Miami, and San Francisco.

Upon his return to Southern California he headed the new technologies division of Paramount Pictures. While there, Nick helped oversee the special effects for the films "Close Encounters of the Third Kind" and "Star Trek-The Movie." In 1983, Nick returned to the consulting field, eventually becoming president of Harrison Price Company.

Nick then joined Warner Bros. as president of its theme park division, overseeing a large portfolio of commercial attractions as well as building new parks in Australia, Germany and Spain. In 2008 he founded and became president of the 501(c)(3) that designed, funded, built and ran the United States Pavilion at the 2010 Shanghai World Expo, the most visited event in history.

Nick continues to do some consulting work, primarily for international clients in China and Latin America. He is an emeritus trustee of his alma mater, Pomona College and is a member of the Economic Round Table of Los Angeles, the Twilight Club and the California Club.

David A. Price AIA, NCARB

Strategic Planning, Design & Project Management
Price Leisure Group Inc.

David Price, President and Founder of the Price Leisure Group, is the son of Disney Legend and IAAPA Hall of Fame recipient Harrison "Buzz" Price. Having grown up in the business, David brings a lifetime of professional experience and relationships in the attractions industry involving family attractions, theme parks, resorts, hotels and restaurants and mixed-use development.

For more than 30 years, he has provided architecture and planning services to private and public sector clients with a special focus in the attractions and entertainment industries. These services included site selection and program analysis, concept development and preliminary design, preparation of construction documents and construction administration.

Today the Price Leisure Group provides strategic planning, design, project management and owner representation services to its valued clients. David's professional background allows him to bring together the talent, technology, chemistry, expertise and experience to support the unique needs of developers, designers, operators and owners in the hospitality, entertainment and attractions industry.

David is a Thomas J. Watson Fellow and has a Master Degree in Architecture from Harvard University. He graduated from Pomona College and studied art and art history at Tyler School of Art in Rome, Italy. He has more than 35 years as a practicing architect and worked extensively with "Buzz" on attractions-related projects in North America and Asia.

David is a long time member of IAAPA and past-president of the Themed Entertainment Association Western Division and continues to serve as a Board Director. He is Vice-President and Board Director for Ryman Arts, an arts education program for talented high school students. David is also Vice-President and Board Director for the Parentis Foundation providing literacy education programs for elementary school children.

He and his wife Alicia, a retired teacher, live in Orange County, California.

www.PriceLeisureGroup.com
dprice@PriceLeisureGroup.com

TEA SATE Academy Day – Silicon Valley, San Jose, CA 2016

David Price at Ryman Arts Student Graduation,
Los Angeles, CA 2016

David Price, TEA Thea Awards Gala, Disneyland, CA

Wife Alicia (mother of our children Ari, Taryn & Janna) & David

CPSIA information can be obtained
at www.ICGtesting.com
Printed in the USA
FSHW02n1449201018

9 780996 750431